Prep L
Camping, Hiking, and Backpacking

A Quick Reference Guide with lists of everything you need to plan for your next adventure or to improvise in your next crisis

Part of the "**Prep Lists Books**" series

Get bonus resource links and book updates at PrepListsBooks.com

Notifications

LINKS: This book is available in both electronic and printed form and both include underlined text links. In electronic books, tap or click on underlined text to open the online resource. In printed books, see the indexed list of link URLs near the end of the book, or visit PrepListsBooks.com > Resources > Links for the same links list.

LEGAL: All information in this book is deemed accurate and reliable as of the date of publication. However, neither the publisher nor the author assume any responsibility for the validity, use, or misuse of any information contained in this publication; and makes no warranties regarding the results of use of information herein. The views expressed in this book should not be taken as expert instruction; the reader is responsible for his or her own actions.

REFERENCES: Mention of third parties or third-party products within this publication is for informational purposes only and constitutes neither a recommendation nor an endorsement. There are some links in this book that the author may benefit from financially—with no change in product price for you. Your support is appreciated.

GEOGRAPHY: Most of the author's personal experience is in northeastern United States. Your local region may feature different plants, animals, topography, safety concerns, and topics of interest.

Published in the United States of America by
Rockatech Multimedia Publishing
ISBN 0-9665432-3-8
RMPeB001-1709.26

Table of Contents: Summary

Use this list of detailed topics to quickly turn to points of interest.

<<< *See Table of Contents: Detail section for specific chapter topics* >>>

About the Author

I am an avid outdoorsman who enjoys being prepared. Most of my personal experience comes from exploring the states where I've lived—New York, Pennsylvania, Maryland, and West Virginia—camping, hiking, hunting, fishing, backpacking, canoeing, trail riding, rock climbing, photographing, video recording, and more.

For some time now, I have developed various checklists of things to remember, projects to do, ideas to plan, or topics to learn more about. Over time, I kept expanding and re-organizing my lists until I thought maybe I should put them all together into some sort of electronic document that I could reference on my cell phone. That is how this book was born—I wrote and compiled it for myself and then adapted it for you. These quick reference lists are not just for kids or newbies; veteran hikers and campers know the value of a detailed checklist to ensure that nothing is forgotten. Whatever you do in the great outdoors, I hope you find the wealth of information in this book as helpful as I have.

This book is the first in a series called "Prep Lists Books." To learn more about future books, and provide feedback on topics and early drafts, please visit PrepListsBooks.com. You can even sign up to be notified when new books or related resources become available. Thanks!

Ron

Ronald E. Kaine

FREE Bonus PDF

Just to say thank you for purchasing my book, I would like to give you a FREE bonus—the **TOOLS** chapter of this Prep Lists book, as a portable quick reference, in a convenient PDF format.

To download PDF go to
RockMediaPub.com/go/ToolsBonus

Table of Contents: Detail

Use this list of detailed topics to quickly turn to points of interest.

Chapter 3. Food 70

Chapter 5. Tools 117

Chapter 6. Skills 161

Chapter 7. Checklists....205

Future Topics

The following topics are planned for future Prep Lists Books, which may be compiled into **Volume 2** of "Prep Lists for Camping, Hiking, and Backpacking," a second edition, or as online resources at PrepListsBooks.com. Please use the online feedback form to let me know what you think about these or other topics that you'd like to see in future books. Thanks.

Destinations

National Parks & National Forests
State Parks & State Forests
Major Hiking Trails
Other Outdoor Attractions

Fun Things to Do

Photography & Videography
Exploring & Geocaching
Educational & Historical
Botany (trees, edible plants, medicinal plants, etc.)
Bush Craft Projects, Games, & Challenges
More Checklists of things to take camping

Family Camping

Safety First for Children
Activities for Kids & Family
Extra Gear for Youngsters & Pets
Family Friendly Foods

Safety

Basic Safety Measures
Keeping Others Informed
Bear and Wild Animals
Recharging from Battery, Solar, Mechanical, or Heat

Introduction

This book of reference material is organized into the following chapters. Originally, these were individual lists for my personal use, which kept growing and multiplying until the idea came to compile them all into a single book. Use the links here or in the Table of Contents to quickly jump to your topic of interest.

Do you need this book of Prep Lists? Of course you do! Consider the following sections—which explain the basic **who**, **what**, **where**, **when**, **why**, and **how** of this book in more detail.

HOW do I use this book?

How can you use this book? Unlike a novel, this informational how-to book is best read topically, not straight from cover to cover. So flip back to the table of contents, tap on a topic of interest, and start learning... as you would any web site, tutorial, or reference guide.

Structure

Chapters and sections are organized into **multiple tables of contents** for quick reference—making it easy to FIND a specific topic or to skim through section headings and IDENTIFY topics of interest. Clicking or tapping these headings and cross-reference links (or using print page numbers) makes Prep Lists Books very easy to use.

Terminology

Throughout this book, there is a clear distinction between "using" a tool and "utilizing" it. Understanding the difference will provide much greater insights for many **common applications** and new methods for **improvising**.

- "USE" indicates an INTENDED purpose, like using a screwdriver to turn screws into wood.
- "UTILIZE" indicates an UNINTENDED purpose, like utilizing a screwdriver to pry open the lid on a can of paint.

Many of the items in this book are featured because of their ability to be utilized well beyond their intended function. This is helpful in two ways: take things with you that have multiple functions, and how to make the best of what you have.

Additional Resources

Visit PrepListsBooks.com to see the following.

- Updates to this book since the last printing
- Links to additional resources on related topics
- Other formats of this book
- Other books in the Prep Lists Books series

WHO reads this book?

Are you a person who should read this book? Probably. Almost anyone who enjoys being outdoors—whether you are on an adventure like camping, hiking, or backpacking; or if you are just out there for work, for play, or an unexpected detour.

The terms "backpacking" or "hiking" used here may also include canoeing, kayaking, horseback riding, trail riding, ATV riding, four-wheeling, snowmobile riding, cross-country skiing, rock climbing, spelunking, and more.

This book is helpful for each of these types of people.

- **Novices** who rarely spend much time outdoors
- **Intermediates** who know the basics of outdoor adventures
- **Experts** who enjoy rustic living far from modern conveniences

Novices

- Get a quick overview of key topics to explore
- Learn about the essentials of outdoor safety or survival
- Understand the importance of resource utilization
- Make checklists of things to be done or packed
- A reference tool to ask better questions of an expert

Intermediates

- A quick refresher of things you've done in the past
- An overview of skills that you can improve upon
- Expand the possibilities for greater comfort and safety
- Streamline and upgrade your preparations

Experts

- Hundreds of ideas for improvising with limited resources
- Learn easier ways to do the same old things
- Save space, weight, or time by multitasking your gear
- Get new ideas that you never thought of before
- A reference tool to teach skills to a novice

WHAT is this book?

This is a book of lists—not detailed instructions. Do not expect this book to teach you how to do everything. However, these lists will almost certainly spark ideas for practical solutions to everyday situations that you never thought of before.

Uses of This Book

- A checklist to see if you have everything you need
- A reminder to add missing items
- A learning tool to acquire new skills
- A refresher to remember forgotten items
- A quick reference of topics to consider
- A textbook to highlight and annotate
- A notebook to capture fresh insights
- A teaching aid for novices
- A mentor to expand your knowledge
- A source of ideas and creativity
- A gift for a birthday or holiday
- A planning tool for each trip or adventure
- A resource for emergency preparedness

Applications for This Book

- Lists of tools to use
- Lists of methods to try
- Lists of gear to acquire
- Lists of features to measure
- Lists of ideas to consider
- Lists of projects to plan

Reading a Prep Lists book is like brainstorming with a room full of experts.

WHEN would I want this book?

When? I'm so glad you asked—I have lists!

When You Need to Learn New Skills

- Training someone to learn the basics: Highlight key topics
- Training yourself in more advanced skills: There is always room for improvement and expansion
- Upgrading your gear: Get the most out of what you carry

When You Are Preparing for a Trip

- Planning your next camping trip: Improved cooking, less gear
- Planning your next backpacking hike: Remember everything, improve your first aid kit
- Arranging for a quick getaway: Use checklists so you can take off on the spur of the moment

When You Want to Plan Ahead

- Organizing your gear for the next season: Add new fire starters, lighter clothing, and better snacks
- Thinking about different scenarios or locations: Consider alternatives and avoid surprises
- Getting ready for a change in seasons (hot or cold): Explore new technologies or trends in comfort

When You Prepare for an Emergency

- Setting up in case of emergency: Keep this book on your cell phone or in your car
- Preparing for a bug out bag: Prioritize the essentials based on your route and needs
- Preparing for a survival situation: The scenarios are endless—plan ahead and be prepared

WHERE do I need this book?

Where might you use this book? Camping, hiking, and backpacking can be done for a variety of reasons, placing you in a wide range of possible locations.

Campsites

- Public campsite in a park
- Group campsite in the woods
- Solo campsite in the forest
- Primitive campsite in the wilderness

The Great Outdoors

Parks, woods, hiking trails, cycling trails, mountain climbing, lake fishing, stream fishing, ski slopes, cross-country ski trails, river rafting or tubing... the list of outdoor activities goes on and on

Emergency Situations

Be prepared by keeping this book in places where you might face an emergency situation.

- Home, office, store, church, club
- Car, truck, camper
- Safe room, storm shelter, basement
- Yard, neighborhood, community, campgrounds

Master the basic skills of camping & hiking and you'll be ready when disaster strikes and survival skills are needed most.

Urban Environments

Outdoor activities also occur in cities and suburbs—in parks and small pockets of woods between neighborhoods.

WHY should I keep this book?

Why the list format? Lists are able to summarize and condense a wealth of information into a very small space. Detail about each item in these lists may already be in your head—you just need to be reminded of it. If you don't know about it already, then you have a starting point to learn more. You don't want to carry around an encyclopedia or dictionary-size manual; you just need a quick reference of topics, ideas, methods, solutions, skills, and tools to get on with your activities.

Lists are a quick reference to accomplish big tasks.

Learn New Things

- See new topics so you can research them and learn more.

  "What is a Trioxane Fuel Bar?"

- Consider new methods, tools, or solutions.

  "How can I start a fire if my matches get soaked?"

- Find out about what others are doing.

  "I want to lighten the weight of my backpack to half of what it is now."

Refresh Your Memory

- Remember options to consider.

  "Which knot should I use for tent stakes?"

- Brainstorm on potential ideas or solutions.

  "I need to capture rain for drinking water. What tools can I utilize?"

- Customize for your personal use.

  "Have I forgotten anything for my trip? We leave in less than an hour."

WHY Go Camping?

For many it's obvious—getting away to the peace and quiet of a more simple life. For others it may seem like more work than it's worth. Whether you're thinking of a quick overnighter while camping next to the SUV, a weekend spent miles from the nearest road, or a family summer vacation, consider these reasons to go camping.

- **Affordable:** Compared to other vacations, the cost of camping is very small—even if you're paying park camping fees.
- **Appreciation:** Camping helps you to see the value in everyday conveniences and modern technology.
- **Bonding:** Spending quality time with family and friends in a relaxed atmosphere may be better than any other experience.
- **Campfires:** There's nothing quite like staring into a dancing fire.
- **Educational:** There's always something to learn with each camping experience, and many parks include exhibits, historic sites, and useful workshops—for the young and old alike.
- **Escape:** Use camping as a great excuse to disconnect and get away from texting, emailing, talking, driving, hurrying, and more.
- **Exciting:** Explore new sights and sounds, encounter wildlife up close, feel your body rev up with refreshing exercise.
- **Memories:** Create wonderful, fun, unique experiences that you'll remember for a lifetime.
- **Peaceful:** It is surprising how your body and your mind respond when you're not stressed out by day-to-day responsibilities.
- **Photography:** Be creative with your camera or cell phone by capturing rare images and videos to share with others.
- **Renew:** Break from your routine, let your mind wander, sleep in, and let your body be refreshed and restored for your return.
- **Self-Confidence:** Sharpen your resilience, courage, and bravery.
- **Prepare:** Update preparations like tents, sleeping bags, hammocks, fire starters, camp food, backpacks, rain gear, hiking books, GPS, geo-caching, and other gear.
- **Skills Refresher:** Remember how to start a fire, fish, hike, climb, boat, backpack, cook over an open fire, & sing campfire songs.

Chapter 1. Fire

Fire: Chapter Intro

Fire is essential to survival when it is cold and dark. Knowing how to build a fire is a key skill for anyone spending time in the outdoors.

Being able to start a fire using various techniques and resources is vitally important—because you don't know what may be available when the need for a fire becomes critical. Remember that you may need to be able to start a fire when it is raining or snowing, in the cold or in the dark, or under the stress of an emergency.

This chapter on fire includes the following topics.

Fire: Purpose & Use

Heat

- Warm yourself, your hands, your feet, and your core
- Dry clothing, footwear, coats, hats, and gear
- Melt snow into water for drinking, cooking, or washing
- Heat rocks to warm boots, tent, or sleeping bag (in or under)
- Heat rocks to create a luxurious steam sauna tent
- Thaw frozen mechanical devices, like bolts and bottle caps
- Incinerate trash, such as cardboard and paper products

Light

- Setting up camp, pitching tent, hanging hammock
- Preparing food, eating, cleaning up (saving battery life)
- Rescue signal—beacon light (nighttime) or smoke (daytime)

Cooking

- Boil, roast, grill, bake, fry, braise, poach, steam, or smoke
- Hot coffee, hot tea, hot soup, hot dogs, or hot marshmallows
- Use smoke and heat to preserve meat

Protection

- Repel bugs (smoke), bear (light), and other wild animals
- Use charcoal to filter water for drinking or use as war paint
- Harden wooden weapons, like spear, gig, and arrow tips
- Sterilize instruments to prevent infection
- Boil water for safe drinking

Comfort

- Place for relaxing, storytelling, and gazing at the flames
- Center or focus of the campsite and entertainment
- Dispel loneliness, calm nerves, or "set the mood"
- Drive an electric generator to recharge cell phone batteries

Fire: Safety

You do NOT want to be the cause of a forest fire. Use an extra measure of common sense when building campfires and if in doubt—be extra safe and take no chances.

This section assumes that you are an adult with an understanding of general fire safety. Children and novices should use additional caution.

When entering a local, state, or national park where you plan to camp or cook out, always look for the color of the Fire Conditions sign and following the corresponding instructions. Visit NPS.gov for details.

Campfire

Consider the following before you build or light a fire in the woods.

Safe Site Selection

- **Avoid** building a fire under tree branches that may catch fire.
- **Avoid** a fire on a steep slope where wind can quickly spread it.

Avoid building a fire on rocks that will leave ugly black marks.

Safe Site Preparation

- Clearly define the fire area to prevent others from walking in it.
- Clear an area around the campfire that cannot burn.
- Consider cutting and rolling away grass turf so fire is on dirt.
- Have plenty of water and a shovel to quickly stop fire spreading.
- Add Sub-Barrier: If the ground is grassy, consider laying down a small tarp or Mylar blanket, covered with dirt, before building your fire—preventing unseen smoldering after you leave.
- Add Perimeter Barrier: If the area looks risky, consider laying a ring of rocks to contain the campfire before you light it.

"Looking" Safe

- **Look up**: Avoid any tree limbs that might catch fire.
- **Look down**: Clear away any dry, flammable, organic material on the ground—including grass, leaves, duff, needles, and sticks.
- **Look around**: Remove any rocks, sticks, or other obstacles that might cause you to trip or stumble around your campfire.

- **Look sharp**: Have a few bottles or bags of water nearby to quickly extinguish any flames that go beyond the intended area—before they have time to spread across grass or leaves.

Safe Fire Building

- Minimize the size of the campfire to keep it under full control.
- The more wind, the smaller the fire must be; or go underground.
- Select quality, hard firewood that minimizes flying sparks.
- Skip the fire if conditions are particularly dry or hazardous.

See It Online: Smokey Bear shows you how to safely build your campfire

Feel the Breeze

For soft breezes, use extra care and build your campfire downwind of a natural windbreak. If it is windy or gusty (over 10 mph), avoid building a campfire or keep it very small (the size of your hand), very well contained (in a pot or in the ground), and very well attended (never walk away).

Safety Reminders

- Never leave a campfire unattended—not even for a minute.
- When finished, coals must be cool enough to handle them.
- Never bury hot coals, which can cause root fires hours later.

Leave No Trace: Leave the campsite looking like no one was there.

Extinguishing Campfires

- As the time draws near to put out the fire, only add small fuel that will burn quickly and completely, and stack unburned fuel together so that it is hotter and more likely to burn to ash.
- Soak the fire area at least an hour before you leave, giving time for it to cool, using less water, and providing greater assurance that there is absolutely no chance for it to come back to life.

Stoves

- Keep stoves on a level surface that cannot be tipped or knocked over, potentially spilling burning fuel across the ground.

- Remember that large alcohol stoves and torches cannot be blown out—they need to be snuffed and deprived of oxygen to extinguish the large flames.

See It Online: Stoves for Cooking Outdoors

More

Warnings and cautions on fire safety could easily fill hundreds of pages and are beyond the scope of this Prep Lists book. If you are new to building fires, it is strongly recommended that you do some research on how to be safe with fire. Here are some places to start.

- SmokeyBear.com
- KidsCamping.com
- PreventWildfireCA.org

Fire: Stage 1. Ignition

Be careful not to confuse "fire starters" with your initial spark, flame, or hot coal. Most commercial or homemade "fire starters" assume that you already have a spark or heat source to light them.

Preparations for Ignition

The following are probably the most common tools to ignite a fire.

Lighters

- Disposable butane lighters are a reliable source of flame that will light most any dry tinder
- Even when the fuel runs out, the flint still creates sparks for you to light suitable tinder or liquid fuel (pry off windscreen)
- Not all lighters are alike—cheap lighters are prone to breaking, leaking, or overheating; rely on quality brands
- For a lighter that requires no fuel, consider an arc lighter; for example, the TekFire Rechargeable USB Lighter
- Pocket torch lighters are more reliable in harsh conditions
- For the ultimate in fire starting lighters, consider the Zippo Emergency Fire Starter kit

Caution: Issues may arise at high altitude or in extreme cold

Buy It Online: Various Lighters for Starting Fires

Matches

- Inexpensive, lightweight, and burn hot
- Must be dry to be effective—consider a waterproof container
- Waterproof, windproof, and stormproof versions are available

Sparks

- Fire Steel or Flint & Steel (Flint sticks are just oversized versions of the little flints found in every cigarette lighter.)
- Ferrocerium Rods
- Stable, long-lasting, multiple use, and works even when wet
- Requires suitable tinder to capture the spark and may need skill to nurse it to flame

- Intense friction between flint rock and high-carbon steel shaves off tiny filings (sparks) that burn at very high temperatures

Natural Ignition

If you find yourself unprepared to start a fire, consider these methods that use only tools found in nature.

Friction from Wood

- Assemble a bow, drill, thong, spindle, plough, saw, or other configurations to generate sufficient heat from friction and tinder to create a small coal
- Then add enough oxygen to the coal for it to burst into flame and light your tinder

Sparks from Rocks

- Look for flint, pyrite, or quartzite rock
- Striking a pointed edged against the back of a pocketknife blade can throw sparks into your tinder

Be sure to practice using these methods to improve your skill—don't just get the tools and expect them to work for you the first time you try.

Emergency: Electricity for Ignition

In most cases—especially in an urban or suburban environment, there are tools around you to assist with fire starting.

- **Electric Cigarette Lighter** in most vehicles
- **Car Battery** and jumper cables or other wire: The spark produced by touching the wires together is hot enough to light most tinder or fuel.
- **9-Volt Battery** or cell phone battery & steel wool: Slide terminals across steel wool, next to tinder, to capture the heat of the burning metal.
- **AA or AAA Battery** with a gum wrapper: Cut foil wrapper to create an hourglass shape, funneling and intensifying the electrical current through a tiny space, heating it to a flame.
- **Improvised Battery** (remember those high school science experiments with potatoes?)

Emergency: Sunlight Refraction for Ignition

Use any of the following to focus bright sunlight on a tiny spot of highly-flammable tinder. To help, consider making your tinder as warm as possible, such as placing it in an aluminum box like a solar oven. This requires bright sunlight, focused on good tinder, with skill and practice to bring a smoking ember to full flame.

Lenses (convex)

- Magnifying lens
- Eye glasses
- Binoculars
- Telescope
- Rifle Scope
- Spotting Scope
- Camera Lens
- Camera Telephoto Lens
- Fresnel lens
- Car headlight/taillight lens
- Clear light bulb filled with water
- Wine goblet filled with water
- Icicle
- Ice lens
- Glass bottle
- Plastic water bottle
- Clear bag of water

Parabolic (concave) Reflectors

- Soda can bottom (polished)
- Flashlight reflector
- Aluminum foil in bowl shape
- Car headlight/taillight reflector
- Steel ladle

Learn more by searching the Internet for "how-to" articles and demonstration videos using search terms from these lists.

Emergency: Other Ignition

- **Road Flares**, which burn hot and bright for half an hour
- **Flare Gun**, flare ammo from a shotgun, or incendiary ammo
- **Shotgun**, by firing cloth wads after removing projectiles
- **Model Rocket Igniters** for a burst of sparks
- **Grinding Tools** to throw sparks
- **Chemicals**—if you are a Chemist, you have many options, like brake fluid and chlorine, or maybe potassium permanganate and glycerin

Fire: Stage 2. Tinder or Accelerant

This stage of tinder or accelerant catches a spark or small flame and intensifies it for extra heat (or for damp fuel). This is where the triangle of fire comes together: heat (spark), fuel (tinder), and oxygen (air). Most of these items are commonly called "fire starters"—although they lack the initial spark or flame needed to light them.

Natural Tinder

You can usually find suitable tinder out in the woods, even in wet weather—saving room in your pack for other essentials, like marshmallows.

- **Bark**: Birch bark, juniper bark, cherry bark
- **Inner Bark**: Particularly aspen, poplar, and cottonwood trees
- **Fungus**: Birch fungus and similar growths often burn well
- **Pine or Fir**: Pull off dead branches, pine cones, bark, needles, sap, or fatwood (sap-soaked wood near branch bases or tree injuries) from standing or dead trees.
- **Wood Shavings**: Use a knife for fuzz sticks, or use pencil sharpener to create shavings
- **Split Wood**: Split into the size of match sticks and pencils; and remember that even wet firewood is dry inside—split open with axe, hatchet, or knife and baton.
- **Dried**: Grass, leaves, thistle heads, weeds, dead plants—these may produce excessive smoke, so not always the best choice
- **Fuzz**: Any dry and fuzzy plants like cattail fuzz, pussy willows, moss, flower petals, or dandelion fuzz

Lint found in your socks or navel can be used as a fire starter. However, I recommend removing the lint before lighting it. :-)

Preps for Tinder

Consider keeping the following things in your pocket, backpack, or survival pack for times when you don't have easy access to natural, dry tinder.

- **Knife**: Use to create fuzz sticks or split wood into small, dry pieces by striking the back of the knife with a baton.
- **Paper**: Newspaper, note paper, food wrapper, lunch bag...
- **Tissue or toilet paper**: flattened roll in a zip-tight plastic bag (for multiple purposes)
- **Pencil Sharpener**: Use to whittle pencil-sized tree branches into small, wood shavings that are easy to light. A pack of several these pencil sharpeners can be purchased at a dollar-type store.
- **Cotton Balls** (Cotton patch, round, swab, cloth, denim, etc.): These light quickly from sparks or small flame, getting damp tinder burning—add accelerant to Cotton Balls (see below) for even better lighting and duration
- **Petroleum Jelly** (Vaseline): Work (or melt) petroleum jelly into a Cotton ball or Cotton patch, this burns 1 to 5 minutes and can be stored in plastic straws or zip-tight plastic bags to keep dry, clean, and isolated—more messy than wax, but easier to light.
- **Paraffin Wax**: Melt and soak paraffin wax into all or part of a Cotton ball or Cotton patch burns 5 to 10 minutes and can be stored in plastic straws or zip-tight plastic bags—not as messy as petroleum jelly, but more difficult to light.
- **Wax & Jelly Balls**: combine the two previous components on each end of a single Cotton ball or Cotton patch for optimal lighting (petroleum jelly end) and extended burn time (paraffin wax end).
- **Paraffin Wax**: Add melted paraffin wax to a small container of Cotton, cardboard, lint, paper, etc. for a long-lasting flame burning 10 to 30 minutes, providing both heat and light—consider a small tin can, Styrofoam egg carton sections, or pill bottles as forms.
- **Jellied Alcohol**: Add to Cotton Balls from heat fuel cans like Sterno, or place lit can under tinder pile if it is damp.

A Cotton ball soaked in jelly or wax can be wrapped in a single-use aluminum foil square to keep protected and handy in your pocket. Cut open with a knife and pull out some cotton fibers to wick the fuel, giving several minutes of burn time.

- **Candle Stubs**: Save the last half inch of any sized candle—with the wick still intact, to provide a steady flame for tinder.

- **Lighter Fluid**: A few tablespoons of fuel burns 30 to 60 seconds and can be stored in a small, glass, eye-dropper bottle.
- **Alcohol Fuel**: A small amount of this non-volatile camp stove fuel is a great accelerant to get damp wood burning. It is also available in a number of other (less expensive) products, like "Gas Line Antifreeze and Water Remover" available in 12-ounce bottles a dollar-type stores.
- **Char Cloth**: This scorched cloth, heated without oxygen to prevent burning, is like charcoal that easily catches low-temperature sparks or helps to bring a small coal to flame.
- **Magnesium**: In shavings or powder, a small pile burns very hot for 10-20 seconds to kick-start your tinder or kindling.
- **Wax Paper**: Fold palm-size piece like an accordion, sprinkle with magnesium shavings, and light with a striker.
- **Trioxane**: Commercial fuel bars like Trioxane are the single greatest method for quickly building a campfire—if you don't mind the price tag.
- **Never Dull**: A commercial polishing product made of soaked cloth fibers, Never Dull lights quickly and burns hot.
- **Duct Tape**: Wad up a small ball of duct tape and light it.

Emergency Tinder

You may have access to one of these items—intended for other purposes, that often work very well when utilized for fire starting.

- **Birthday Candles**, especially the "trick" candles that stay lit
- **Cleaning Products** made with alcohol
- **Clothing**, Cotton shirt patch, denim threads, etc.
- **Coconut Oil**, or Crisco oil, used like petroleum jelly
- **Cologne or perfume** made with alcohol
- **Cutting or Welding Torch** with acetylene gas
- **Dryer Lint**, pocket lint, sock lint, Cotton fringe
- **Disposable Baby Diapers**, or a small cutting from one
- **Feminine Napkins**, pads, or similar products
- **Grease**, from food or machines like car, snowmobile, tractor
- **Greasy Foods** like corn chips, potato chips, peanuts, croutons

- **Gunpowder**, from shotgun shells or rifle/pistol cartridges
- **Hand sanitizer** with alcogel (62% alcohol)—consider soaking Cotton balls, lint, or tinder with common sanitizer gel (available at a dollar-type store)
- **Lip Balm**, like ChapStick, mixed with lint or cloth
- **Petroleum Jelly**, like Vaseline, especially when added to cloth, lint, paper, Cotton
- **Propane** torch, tank, heater, or grill
- **Sanitizing Alcohol Wipes** in individually-wrapped foils, these wipe cloths burn about 10-20 seconds each
- **Shoe parts**, rubber sole section, plastic logo, lace
- **Tissue or toilet paper**, for multiple purposes
- **Ultra-fine Steel Wool**, for electrical sparking
- **Wax**, often used for skis, surfboards, or candles
- **Anything Else** like paint, lubricant, auto fluid, oil, fuel additive, starting fluid, adhesive, glue, epoxy, cleaning solvent, stain, varnish, thinner, gunpowder, bug repellent, hairspray, hair mousse, fingernail polish remover, cooking oils, disinfectant sprays, distilled spirits, or even garden chemicals.

Visit Backpacker.com > Survival Skills > Starting a Fire > Tinder Finder online for help finding tinder in your geographical region.

Fire: Stage 3. Kindling

The kindling stage adds or maintains heat from burning tinder to light your primary fuel—transitioning into a full campfire. Most kindling fuel will be small sticks or split wood—about the size of pencils.

Collect an armful of kindling BEFORE lighting your campfire. If high-quality kindling and fuel are available, less may be needed. If you think some time and effort will be required to get the fire going (like after a heavy rain), it is better to collect too much kindling than to not have enough on hand. Have enough kindling prepared to avoid needing to start over.

Identification

All kindling wood is:

- **Dead**: No green leaves or green bark on it
- **Hard**: Not mushy, soggy, or rotten
- **Loud**: Produces a sharp crack sound when broken
- **Light**: Weighs less than wet or rotten wood of similar size

Sources

Consider these kindling sources.

- **Bark**: from birch, cherry, or other smooth-barked trees
- **Branches**: ¼" to ½" thick, up to one foot long
- **Pine Cones**: large, dry, brown, open (these will be smoky)
- **Split**: split from blocks of wood into the size of pencils
- **Rolled Paper**: tightly rolled into finger-sized logs

This list of ideas is just to get you started. Learn more by searching the Internet for articles and demonstrations using search terms from these lists.

Fire: Stage 4. Fuel

Fuel provides the long-term combustion in your campfire.

- Softwood: minimum three to five square feet per hour
- Hardwood: minimum one to two square feet per hour

TIP: Break up all of your fuel into one to two-foot lengths BEFORE you light your campfire. Wedging branches between two tree trunks that are a few inches apart gives you the leverage to do this quickly and easily—without any additional tools.

In addition to just using your bare hands, a variety of tools may be used to collect and cut firewood, including saws, axes, and more.

Only cut wood from dead trees or limbs—nothing living with green on it.

Medium Fuel

This includes branches and split wood about an inch thick.

- Produces quick cooking coals
- Perks up a fire that is waning
- Dries out larger, damper fuel

Large Fuel

This is wrist to arm-sized wood—especially hardwoods.

- Burns slowly
- Throws lots of heat
- Produces long-lasting coals

Huge Fuel

Big logs—more than a few inches thick—burn or smolder for many hours, rarely burn up completely, and are difficult to fully extinguish. Most experts recommend not using these unless you will be at the same site for multiple days—or when needed for survival.

Backpacker.com > Survival Skills > Starting a Fire
is a great resource for more information on this topic.

Fire: Application

Fire Lay Methods

Before you start building your fire, you should decide which type of fire lay you need, given your conditions and use of the fire.

- **Teepee (or Tipi)**: Quick, easy, flexible, focused heat
- **Log Cabin**: Stable, burns more slowly, provides better coals
- **Top-Down Log Cabin (Council Fire, Top-Lighter)**: Burns very slowly with minimal maintenance
- **Lean-To**: Best accommodating for wind and awkward fuel
- **Hunter's**: Built between two parallel logs provides better wind control and an easy platform for pots & pans
- **Dakota Fire Pit**: Built underground in one end of a U-shaped tunnel, the controlled air flow make this very hot, well-contained, and easy to arrange a pot or pan.
- **Hybrid**: Combining variations of any of the above
- **Finnish**: Stacked logs for very long burns
- **Keyhole**: Combining a larger/circular area for the fire, and a smaller/rectangular area for dragging hot coals for cooking
- **Star (Indian)**: Burning the ends or middles of long logs (like the spokes of a wheel) and rearranging them as they burn through—into shorter logs

Visit PrepListsBooks.com for links to "how-to" articles and demonstration videos.

A One-Stick Fire

After a heavy rain, most natural materials will be too wet to make a fire—unless you expose the dry wood inside logs and branches. Learn how to use a knife and a baton to create your own tinder (shavings), kindling (feather or fuzz sticks), and fuel (split wood) from a single stick of wood. Using this method eliminates the need for a heavy axe, a big saw, or any other equipment.

Fire: Chapter Review

Chapter Summary

Is there anything you'd like to review again?

- **Purpose** & use for fire
- **Safety** when using fire
- Stage 1. **Ignition** to start a fire
- Stage 2. **Tinder** or Accelerant to start a fire
- Stage 3. **Kindling** to start a fire
- Stage 4. **Fuel** to maintain a fire
- **Application** to build a campfire

Chapter Action Steps

☐ Always practice safety when working with fire.

☐ Prepare fire starting tools to keep ready-to-go in your pack.

☐ Practice new fire starting methods so when the need arises, you already have experience using them.

☐ Experiment with different fire layout methods to see what works best for your camping needs.

☐ Build a Dakota Fire as a new challenge to boil water.

The trouble with doing something right the first time
is that nobody appreciates how difficult it was. ☺

Next Chapter

While fire is often an essential for camping or surviving in the woods—especially when it is cold outside, being able to enough drink (safe, healthy) fluids is even more important for maintaining your wellbeing. See the next chapter for great information about finding, transporting, and purifying water to drink.

Chapter 2. Water

Water: Chapter Intro

Water is essential to live and for your good health. Plan on at least a gallon of water per person per day—depending on temperature, age, and physical condition. This does not include water needed for cooking, cleaning, bathing, or pets. Ideally, you would take bottled or clean tap water with you, but the weight or space needed is often limiting. So here are some ideas for obtaining drinkable water away from home. This chapter on water includes the following topics.

Water: Finding

To replace or supplement the fresh water that you brought with you, here are some ideas for finding water in the wilderness.

Remember that all water found in nature should be purified before drinking.

On the Move

- Go downhill into valleys to find streams and ponds
- Listen for running water from distant rapids or waterfalls
- Follow the beds of seasonal streams to find water pools
- Follow rocky canyons to find pools of rainwater
- Follow merging game trails & tracks that may lead to waterholes
- In dry or rocky areas, look for green plants to find water
- In a dry riverbed, look for green plants to locate damp earth
- In a dry riverbed, look for drinking holes dug by thirsty animals
- Bees and flies must live close to water

When possible, take water from a moving stream or waterfall rather than a standing pool or pond, which is much more likely to have contaminants.

Characteristics

For the best quality—or least contaminated water, look for these characteristics.

- Moving or flowing rather than standing or stagnating—this makes it less hospitable to pathogens.
- Bubbling, gurgling, or rippling rather than smooth flowing—this oxygenation helps to purify it.
- Passed through vegetation like reeds, grass, and moss—this does extensive filtering of phosphorous, nitrates, and foreign matter.
- Near the top of standing water—this layer is the most exposed to the ultraviolet rays of sunlight, which kills germs.

Extraction

- **Drips:** Use a string and bottle to collect a slow drip from a cliff.
- **Straw:** Create a straw to suck water out of cracks and crevices.

- **Well:** Dig a small well in a dry stream bed to find a lower water table; water often continues to flow beneath the surface.
- **Dew:** Soak a cotton cloth or t-shirt with morning dew on grass, trees, and other plants; then squeeze the water from the cloth into your mouth (or container) and repeat. You can use your hands or tie to your ankles and simply walk through wet grass.
- **Transpiration:** tightly wrap a plastic bag over a green, leafy tree branch or any leafy vegetation in direct sunlight to trap moisture as it evaporates and condenses on the inside of the plastic bag. If you injure the limbs, more water will be pumped to that area. A small rock at the bottom will help collect water. 24 hours may produce one cup of water.
- **Evaporation:** Create a solar still to extract moisture from most dirt, mud, dirty water, urine, etc. The evaporated condensate is also purified and ready to drink.
- **Vines:** Clear liquid seeping from cut vines is likely drinkable. Avoid if liquid is milky or cloudy.
- **Crush:** Squeeze pulpy plants (like cactus) to extract water.
- **Snow:** Collect clean snow and melt (or boil) before drinking.

Vegetation: If your purpose for looking for water is to drink it, remember that many fruits, berries, and vegetables have water in them.

Collection

Collect rain water by redirecting from a large surface to a narrow collection point.

- Spread or hang a tarp, raincoat, jacket, blanket, tent, or other material with a valley in the middle (A "V" shape) to direct rain water into a container (remember to account for wind direction).
- If you don't have a container to store the rainwater, tie ends of your collector sheeting up so that it holds water in the middle
- Find a location under the trees where rain water is drizzling the most and place your container under it.
- Construct a large "roof" of wood, leaves, and grass to capture and direct rain water into a container (or your mouth).

- Hang large, absorbent material (blanket, clothing, bed sheets, etc.) to soak up falling rain and wring into a container—repeating as needed.
- Gather snow and ice that will melt by the fire—ideally in a cloth sack like a pillowcase, which can be suspended over a container to collect the dripping water as it melts.

A 10' × 12' tarp can collect over 50 gallons of water from one inch of rain.

Water: Transporting

OK, so you found water—but what if you need to use this water somewhere else, perhaps somewhere far away? Consider these options for moving water (and other liquids).

Safety First: Before lighting a campfire, be sure to have plenty of water within reach to quickly stop any unexpected spreading.

Plan Ahead

Take these lightweight items with you for carrying water.

- Plastic Water Bottles
- Canteen
- Water Bladder
- Aluminum Foil
- Zip-Tight Plastic Bags
- Trash Bags
- Food Containers

Improvised

Consider these ideas to create your own water containers.

Drinking Cup: fold a large, green leaf (maple, oak, etc.) into a funnel shape to hold a few ounces of water for drinking.

Plastic Liners: Place watertight garbage bag (or multiple bags for added durability) or plastic sheets inside another container to give it strength:

- Backpack
- Fanny pack
- Duffle bag
- Bucket or pail
- Basket
- Hat
- Sleeping bag
- Pillowcase
- Burlap bag

- Pants
- Sweatshirt
- Ditty bag
- Folding lawn chair bags
- Shoes or boots
- Cardboard boxes

*Remember that you will need a way to carry these heavy containers—
for example, tying two bags together and balancing them over your shoulder,
or attaching to a pole carried by two people.*

In Nature: Utilize eggs, gourds, folded birch bark, folded leaves. Use mud inside a bark bowl to make it watertight.

Folded tarp: A three square foot tarp can be folded into a bucket with a handle to carry over the shoulder.

Rubber/Plastic Tubes: Cut into a bucket shape from an inner tube, an inflatable raft, a rubber boat, or inflatable pool toys.

Condom: Carry a jumbo-size, non-lubricated latex condom in your first-aid kit or fanny pack to carry a gallon of water.

From the Junk Yard, River's Edge, or Seashore: Look for useful items along the side of busy roads, in trash bins, behind retail stores or industrial facilities, etc. Water-carrying containers may include: plastic shopping bags, trash bags, aluminum cans, plastic water bottles, 2-liter soda bottles, milk jugs or cartons, laundry detergent bottles, tin cans, glass jars, trash cans, flower pots, food storage containers, and more.

Water: Purifying

Always filter and boil (or treat) water to be used for drinking or cooking—as most natural sources likely contain dangerous or unfamiliar parasites, germs, and bacteria that can make you sick. Bad guys that may be found in surface water include: Hepatitis A, Giardia, Shigella, E.coli, Salmonella, Campylobacter jejuni, coliform, cholera, and viruses

However, even muddy, smelly water can be made drinkable with proper filtering and boiling—but avoid any bitter or alkali-tasting water as it is poisonous and can only be treated by distillation.

===V===

QUICK TIP: While this chapter includes many methods to purify water that may have biological or chemical contamination, here is my three-step approach for most water found in the woods.

- **1. Rough filter** (cloth, coffee filters, sand): remove debris
- **2. Fine filter** (charcoal, carbon, ceramic): remove chemicals
- **3. Bleach** (or BOIL if I already have a fire going): remove germs
  ~10 drops/gal of Chlorine bleach, wait 30 mins to kill everything

===Λ===

This section on purifying water includes the following methods.

<<< Tap or click for quick navigation to one of these topics >>>

1. Filtering Water

Several types of filters can be used as the first stage in water purification or as a better-than-nothing alternative before drinking questionable water.

Prepared Filters

- Keep a stash of coffee filters or dust masks in your pack

Remember these items have multiple uses if needed.

- Water bottles with built-in filters can slowly process water while you hike to your destination

Remember to replace filters frequently to maintain effectiveness.

- Filtered straws can be purchased for use in an emergency

See It Online: Lifestraw Water Filter

Natural Filters

When possible, use water that has already been filtered by nature.

- Passed through vegetation like reeds, grass, moss, etc.
- Moving or flowing rather than standing or stagnating
- Bubbling, gurgling, or ripping rather than smooth flowing

Dirt Filter

You can do the following with no tools but your hands and maybe a stick or a rock.

- About five to ten feet away from the edge of a pond or swamp water, dig a hole about two feet wide and a foot deep.
- As you are digging, water from the surrounding soil will seep into your hole. Bail out this water two or three times, which will likely be muddy or discolored.
- By then, the water that seeps into your hole will be clear and drinkable—because the ground itself has filtered the water.
- Note, however, that this method will NOT filter out any chemical toxins—so look around at nearby vegetation and signs of wildlife drinking in this area to ensure that it is clear of pollution.

Improvised Filters

Do the following to remove visible impurities like dirt, plants, sand, mud, or general cloudiness.

- Strain water through a handkerchief, t-shirt, cloth, paper towel, coffee filter, or dust mask.
- These makeshift filters can be placed over the mouth of a bottle or canteen to filter water as it passes in or out of the container.
- A plastic bottle can also be cut into a funnel to hold your filter materials.
- Repeat filtering with finer materials or more layers to improve quality.

Create a Charcoal Filter

- Create a funnel-shaped container that has input and output, like a 2-liter plastic bottle with the bottom cut off.
- In this container, layer fine charcoal dust, cloth, and sand.
- After passing water through improvised filters (see above), pour water through this do-it-yourself multi-layered filter to remove very fine particulate matter and most parasites.
- For 100% effectiveness with removing germs, boil your filtered water to ensure that it is safe to drink.

Reliability: Very few filters, store-bought or homemade, will remove 100% of all undesirable contaminants. Heat (boiling) is more reliable.

2. Boiling Water

Without a high-quality filter, boiling water is the best and most reliable method of purifying water for drinking, removing all living microorganisms. To be extra cautious, some might say to boil water for 10 minutes or more. The key is to raise the temperature above 160 degrees long enough to kill all germs and parasites—which doesn't take very long. The CDC recommends boiling for one minute. Most experts agree that a full, rolling boil is sufficient.

Poor Taste: Boiling water releases air from the water, giving it a flat, unpleasant taste. Drizzling clean water between two containers (like you see in a fish aquarium) can infuse air back into the water and restore some of the taste. Even better is to mix in flavoring like powdered lemon juice or fruit-flavored drink mix.

Direct Heat

Method 1: Place water in a metal container (any container that won't burn in a fire) and boil over a fire or bed of hot coals.

- Containers might include: beverage can, tin can, pot, canteen, aluminum foil shaped into a bowl, etc.
- Depending on the size of your fire, you should be able to bring it to a boil within a few minutes.

Method 2: Place water in any container and place hot rocks from a fire into the water-filled container

- Containers might be made of plastic, bark, hide, cloth, glass, seashell, bamboo, coconut, or anything else that could not be placed over a fire. Plan ahead by packing several lightweight turkey-sized oven bags, which hold a gallon of water.
- Heat large rocks (that will still fit into your container of water) in a fire for about 10-15 minutes, then drop them one-at-a-time into your water for about 20 to 30 seconds each. You should be able to flash boil your water within a couple of minutes.

Caution: Boiling water does NOT remove things like chlorine, gasoline, ammonia, herbicides, pesticides, arsenic, lead, mercury, etc. Use a charcoal filter for these.

Plastic Bottle

If a plastic bottle is the only thing you have to hold water, there are still options for using it and heat to purify water. A word of caution, however, in that a slight misjudgment in heat or placement may ruin an otherwise good water container.

- Completely fill the bottle with water, cap it tightly, and place the full bottle in or above some hot coals. The water inside and lack of air should prevent the water from boiling and the plastic from melting. Your goal is to get the water above 160 degrees for several minutes.
- Suspend a plastic water bottle just above flames or coals so that the water inside keeps the plastic from melting.
- Leave the water bottle in bright sunshine for several hours to help kill any bacteria or parasites from the sun's heat, light, and ultraviolet rays.

Poisons: Boiling water kills harmful pathogens, but does not remove chemicals, toxins, or poisons like oils or metals.

3. Distilling Water

Using water evaporation in a still—whether commercial or improvised, is best for making drinkable water from the worst sources, like the following.

- Sea water
- Polluted water
- Industrial runoff water
- Urine

Heat is needed to increase the rate of evaporation. This heat may come from the sun (solar), from a fire (wood, stove, etc.), or any other heat source. The heat can just be warm enough to encourage evaporation, or hot enough to create steam. Plan ahead by packing several lightweight turkey-sized oven bags.

Stills can be created in a number of ways. Each has the following basic components.

- A container of unclean water
- A heat source to accelerate evaporation or create steam
- A means to capture evaporated water
- A clean collection container

Consider the following ideas to distill unsafe water and make it drinkable.

Bottle Trough Still

Cut bottom off of a clean, plastic bottle—the larger the better. Roll up the bottom edge so that it curls inward, creating a trough around the inside, about an inch deep. If needed, use heat from a flame to help mold the plastic. Place this still, with cap in place, over something wet and in direct sunlight. If needed, use string to suspend this still over unclean water that is being heated. As evaporation (or steam) rises and condenses on the sides of the bottle, it will collect in the trough. To drink, twist off the cap and drink like any water bottle. Repeat as needed.

Hourglass Bottle Still

Fill a water bottle one-third full of unpurified water. Tape another bottle to this bottle at the mouth, so that together they look like an hourglass. Please these bottles in direct sunlight at a slight angle so that evaporated water from the lower side can cool and collect in the upper side.

Tree Branch Transpiration

Tightly wrap a plastic bag around a leafy tree branch (or any leafy vegetation) and let sit several hours—until evaporated water from leaves collects in the bottom of the bag.

Wide-Mouth Jar

Position a large, clear, glass or plastic jar over a container of unclean water in a manner that allows evaporated water to collect on the inside of the large jar and trickle down into a clean collection container. You may need several of these to produce enough distilled water.

Plastic Bag

Much like the jar described above—with some effort, you can set up a large, clear, plastic bag—with unclean water in the bottom and inflated or propped up to direct distilled water out the side. Multiple bags will multiply the amount of water collected.

Hole in the Ground

- Dig a large hole in the ground, about a foot deep and 3 feet wide
- Place a large container of unclean water in the hole
- Place in the center of the hole a clean collection container
- Cover the hole with a clear plastic sheet and secure around the edges with rocks or dirt
- Place a small weight in the middle of the plastic sheet so that condensation that collects on the bottom of the sheet will drip into the clean collection container.

Large Bucket, Drum, or Pool

- Place unclean water in the large container

- Place in the center of the large container a small, clean collection container, which may need to be weighed down to keep it from in position
- Cover the large container with a clear plastic sheet and secure tightly to the rim
- Place a small weight in the middle of the plastic sheet so that condensation that collects on the bottom of the sheet will drip into the clean collection container.

Capture Steam

- Prepare a place to boil water—over a stove, campfire, candle, etc.
- Using an inverted funnel-shaped device, capture steam from the boiling water into a long, clean tube that directs the steam—as it cools and condensates into distilled water, into a clean collection container.
- Alternatively, tie large leaves, bottles, sheets of metal, or panes of glass above the rising steam that will collect the cooled vapor and drip into your container.
- Additionally, you can position cloth, t-shirt, towel, sponge, etc. over the rising steam to collect the moisture. When saturated, wring them out into a container.

See more online at HowStuffWorks.com > Wilderness Survival

4. Treating Water with Chemicals

Liquid Chlorine Bleach

Unscented household bleach is one of the best, easiest, cheapest, and most readily available products for water treatment. It kills bacteria, parasites, and viruses, and most any living microorganism in water before breaking down and going away. However, it is less effective with protozoa, Crypto, or Giardia, so use caution if that might be in your area.

Before treating the water with bleach, collect clear or filtered water in a container. If the water is still cloudy, wait for sediment to settle to the bottom and pour into another container (stopping before the sediment is poured). Repeat until water is clear. Using a piece of cloth over the mouth of your container also helps.

After treating with bleach, mix well and let sit for half an hour. Immediately after treating, water should have a slight smell of chlorine—if it does not, apply more bleach, mix well, and wait another ten minutes.

*Remember to disinfect the bottle top, cap, and threads—
do this by shaking with the cap fitting loosely to spread the bleach.*

- Use 1 or 2 drops of bleach to treat a 16 oz. bottle of water.
- Use 8 to 16 drops of bleach (or about ¼ teaspoon) to disinfect one gallon of water (double for muddy or cloudy water).
- If treated water is relatively clear and has a chlorine smell, it is disinfected, harmless, and fully drinkable.
- Bleach is powerful; 1 tsp treats a 5-gallon bucket, so don't overdo.

Remember to also disinfect your cookware, eating utensils, toothbrush, & hands.

- Bleach that is more than a year old loses about half of its potency, so adjust the dosage accordingly.
- After water has been treated with bleach, the smell of chlorine will go away in a day or two—much like with city water.
- Water in large tanks can be treated regularly about once or twice a month to keep it free of contaminants. Remember that bleach

does not stay chemically active for more than a few days and that most germs need sunlight to grow.
- A one-ounce eyedropper bottle of bleach, kept in a backpack or survival kit, can treat over 100 gallons of water.

Caution: Treating water with bleach does NOT remove things like chlorine, gasoline, ammonia, herbicides, pesticides, arsenic, lead, mercury, etc. Use a charcoal filter to help remove these.

Dry Chlorine Powder

Also known as calcium hypochlorite, dry chlorine powder is used mostly for swimming pools. As a powder, it has an extended shelf life, and may be stored up to 10 years with minimal degradation.

IMPORTANT: After treating water with dry chlorine powder, let the water stand for 24 hours before drinking.

- For chlorinating water in large tanks, use ¼ ounce by weight per 250 gallons.
- For chlorinating a 55-gallon drum of water, use 1/20 ounce (one level teaspoon).
- A 5-gallon bucket needs 1/200 ounce (a tiny pinch)
- A one-quart canteen needs 1/4000 ounce (just a few individual grains of the powder).
- A small, one-ounce vial of chlorine powder, kept in a backpack or survival kit, can treat 4000 canteens of water.

Iodine

Most iodine bottles include instructions for use. If yours doesn't, use 10 to 12 drops for one gallon of water. Increase the dosage if the water is cloudy or of questionable quality. Mix well and let stand for half an hour before using. Iodine does leave an unpleasant aftertaste.

Treating water with iodine is much like treating with bleach; see the Liquid Chlorine Bleach section above for cautions and effectiveness.

Other Treatments

Follow instructions carefully for these alternative treatments, and remember to consider the shelf life for potency.

- **Water Purification Tablets**—Usually either chlorine or iodine
  > Potable Aqua Chlorine Dioxide Water Purification Tablets
- **Iodine Crystals**—A concentrated form of iodine
- **Potassium Permanganate**—A few potassium permanganate crystals disinfects several cups of water, leaving a light pink color. Bonus: add a few more crystals to make an antiseptic (dark pink), and a few more to make an antifungal treatment (darker pink).
- **Stabilized Oxygen**—New products on the market include Aerobic 07, Aerox, Aquagen, Dynamo 2, and Genesis 1000
- **Mechanical Devices**—For more information, search Amazon.com about various mechanical treatment products
- **Desalination**—Removing salt from sea water (see 3. Distilling Water section earlier in this chapter)

Learn more by searching the Internet
for "how-to" articles and demonstration videos.

5. Treating Water with Light

When filtered water in clear bottles (glass or plastic) is exposed to direct sunlight for six hours (or up to 48 hours in clouded sunlight), the heat and ultraviolet (UV) radiation of the sunlight kill protozoan parasites and bacteria, and inactivates most viruses.

NOTE: Unfiltered or cloudy water requires more time and is less effective—adding a pinch of salt can help to decontaminate the floating particles.

Similarly, you can purchase UV water purifier lights to immerse into a bottle of water to purify it much more quickly and reliably.

Here are some benefits to using UV light to disinfect water.

- Economical—treating large quantities for very little cost
- More effective against viruses than chlorine
- No by-products
- No change in taste, odor, or pH
- No chemicals added
- No overdosing problems
- No removal of beneficial minerals.
- Safe to use

Caution: Treating water with UV light does NOT remove things like chlorine, gasoline, ammonia, herbicides, pesticides, arsenic, lead, mercury, etc. Use a charcoal filter to help remove these.

Have you ever wondered what germs are in unclean water? Here's a list of common microorganisms that are destroyed by UV light.

- Bacillus anthracis
- Bacteriophage (E. Coli)
- Baker's yeast
- Corynebacterium diphtheriae
- Dysentary bacilli (diarrhea)
- Escherichia coli (diarrhea)
- Hepatitis
- Influenza
- Legionella pneumophilia
- Mycobacterium tuberculosis

- Poliovirus (poliomyelitis)
- Pseudomonas aeruginosa
- Salmonella (food poisoning)
- Salmonella paratyphi (enteric fever)
- Salmonella typhosa (typhoid fever)
- Shigella dysentariae (dysentery)
- Shigella flexneri (dysentery)
- Staphylococcus epidermidis
- Streptococcus faecaelis
- Vibro commo (cholera)

Water: Chapter Review

Chapter Summary

Remember these considerations for potable drinking water.

- **Finding** water in the woods
- **Transporting** water from the source
- **Purifying** water: filtering, boiling, distilling, chemical treatment, UV light treatment

Chapter Action Steps

☐ Make sure your backpack or first aid kit has something to purify water, like bleach, iodine tablets, or a UV light.

☐ Practice building a multi-layer water filter using natural materials like rocks, sand, vegetation, and charcoal.

☐ Consider getting an eye-dropper type medicine bottle to carry chlorine bleach with a label indicating "16 drops/gallon".

☐ If you find this book useful, consider writing a brief review for it on Amazon.com. I'd also like to see your feedback for future books in this Prep Lists Books series. Thank you!

Gag Gift: A can of dehydrated water. Just add water! ☺

Next Chapter

Now that you have water ready to drink, let's eat! Use the next chapter on food to make preparations quick and easy. Browse topics for new ideas, review recipes for new favorites, and learn more about your cooking options.

Chapter 3. Food

Food: Chapter Intro

Everyone has different tastes, preferences, resources, time, temperature, tools, and more that affect what food might work best on your next trip to the woods. Here are some quick and easy ideas to consider.

REMINDER: This is not a recipe book; it is a list of ideas to help you prepare.

This chapter on food includes the following topics.

Food: Basic Preparation

Consider these standards on any hiking trip to support or supplement your other meals and snacks.

Condiments

- Ketchup & mustard individual packets
- Hot sauce packets
- BBQ sauce packets
- Mayo & relish packets
- Salt & pepper packets
- Sugar & sweetener packets
- Creamer & dried milk packets/tubs
- Salad dressing packets (mix with foraged greens or use as a meat marinade)
- Oil or bacon grease for frying or flavor

Drinks

- Powdered drink mix for flavor, plus sugar as needed
- Lemon powder packets (for cooking or for drinking)

These are great to improve the taste of local water after purifying

Pills & Medications

- Vitamins, Fiber, Nutritional Supplements
- OTC/Non-Prescription Medications
- Prescription Medications

Safety

- For perishable meats (jerky, sausages, pepperoni), use 4-ounce packages or smaller to avoid spoiling and bear-attracting odors.
- For any wrapper or container that smells of food or grease, burn or wrap in an air-tight container until it can be burned to avoid attracting bear and small critters while you sleep.
- When backpacking, consider keeping all food in a rigid, air-tight container that keeps food from being squashed, keeps it dry, and

reduces odors that might attract bear, bugs, or other wild animals. Ideas to consider for this include a waterproof dry box used for boating, or an ammo box used for firearms.
- At night, place ALL food, wrappers, and smelly trash into a plastic bear bag or cinch sack, and tie up in a tree to keep out of reach from wild animals. Even if you can't get it up out of reach, keep it away from where you are sleeping.

Tips and Time Savers

- Measure and chop all meal ingredients ahead of time and pack in separate zip-tight plastic bags with labels.
- Use emptied zip-tight plastic bags for trash containers.
- Instead of packing and protecting eggs in the shell, crack them at home and keep in a zip-tight plastic bags or a water bottle.
- Prepare meals ahead of time and freeze in portion sizes that will defrost in time for your next meal time. (Several smaller portions thaw more quickly than one large portion.)
- Frozen meat and cans of frozen juice in a cooler keeps other items cold without extra ice.
- Apply inexpensive liquid soap to bottom of any cookware before placing on fire; this makes cleanup much easier.
- Pitas, English muffins, or bagels pack better than sliced bread
- Leather work gloves double as an oven mitt to handle hot items
- Consider a vacuum sealing system to keep foods fresher longer

See more about plastic bags in the section named
***Zip-tight Plastic Bags** in Chapter 5*

Tools

Cooking Oil

Along with cooking, consider these ideas for using and utilizing this all-purpose tool, whether vegetable oil, olive oil, peanut oil, or any other cooking oil in the Tools: Cooking Supplies > **Cooking Oil** section in Chapter 5.

Aluminum Foil

In addition to cooking with aluminum foil, consider these ideas for using and utilizing this all-purpose tool in the Tools: Cooking Supplies > **Aluminum Foil** section in Chapter 5.

Food: No Cooking

Meats/Protein

Small packages recommended, less than 3 ounces each

- Jerky
- Sausages
- Pepperoni
- Tuna Pouches
- Chicken Pouches

For safety from wild animals and to avoid scavenger animals, remember to properly dispose of smelly containers after use.

- Nuts & Seeds: peanuts, cashews, pine nuts, macadamia nuts
- Peanut Butter in jars, packets, or zip-tight plastic bag
  ...mix with Jelly Packets on Crackers or in sandwiches
- Hard Cheese

Vegetables

- Baby Carrots
- Broccoli Heads
- Cauliflower Heads
- Celery (great with peanut butter)

Starch & Sweets

- Fresh Fruit
- Breads, Buns, Muffins, Pastries, Bagels, etc.
- Trail Mix (GORP)
- Granola Bars or Mixes
- Energy Bars, Protein Bars
- Fruit Cups, Applesauce Cups, Pudding Cups
- Dried Fruit
- Dry Cereal Cups
- Crackers, Peanut Butter Crackers, Pretzels, Snacks
- Cookies, S'mores kit or chocolate/marshmallow/grahams
- Roast starburst candies over an open campfire

Drinks

Adding flavor to lukewarm water makes it more enjoyable.

- Kool-Aid
- Crystal Light
- Gatorade Drink Mix
- Punch Drink Mixes
- Lemonade
- Tang
- Nido dried milk mix (great with breakfast cereal)

Remember that you need to drink more than usual when hiking outdoors.

Food: Just Add Hot Water

Drinks

Adding flavor to hot water makes it much more enjoyable.

- Hot tea, in individually wrapped tea bags, in hundreds of flavors (remember sweetener and creamer if needed)
- Hot chai spice powder mix
- Hot chocolate packets

Meals with Hot Water

For many of these food items, you can simply pour the hot water into the pouch or heavy-duty freezer zip-tight plastic bag so that there's no dirty dishes to clean. Use a hat, shirt, or glove to protect your hand from the heat.

- Oatmeal packets & cups
- Instant soup packets & cups
- Ramen noodles packages
- Pasta sauce packets (consider with noodles or meats)
- Instant Potatoes (box, cup, packet)
- Meals-Ready-to-Eat (MRE) - typically freeze dried
- Make your own freeze-dried meals

To include meat in any of these recipes,
freeze in a separate bag with ice to keep safe for several hours.
If you need it to wait overnight or longer, try using freeze dried or canned meat.

Prep Gallon-sized freezer zip-tight plastic bag with seasonings & bouillon (and maybe noodles), ready to add fresh fish (or game meat) and boiling water for a quick and tasty soup.

Meals in a Cup

Potato Soup

Prepare the following in a plastic bag. When ready to eat, pour about half a cup of the mix into a cup with boiling water, stir, and wait a few minutes.

- 2 cups instant mashed potatoes
- 1.5 cups dry milk
- 2 tablespoons chicken bullion
- 2 teaspoons salt
- 2 teaspoons dried onion
- Big pinches of seasonings like pepper, parsley, thyme, turmeric

Tortilla Soup

Prepare the following in a plastic bag. When ready to eat, pour into a cup with boiling water, stir, and wait a few minutes.

- 3 tablespoons crushed tortilla chips
- 2 tablespoons instant rice
- 1 tablespoon Instant Vegetable Soup mix
- 1 teaspoon chicken bouillon
- 1/8 teaspoon each of onion powder, garlic powder, cumin

Mexican Chicken and Hominy Soup

Prepare the following in a plastic bag. When ready to eat, pour into a cup with boiling water, stir, and wait a few minutes.

- 1/3 cup shredded chicken
- 1/4 cup jarred salsa Verde
- 1 teaspoon chicken bullion
- 1 teaspoon cumin
- 1/4 cup canned hominy
- 1/4 cup canned pinto beans
- 1/4 cup coleslaw mix or shredded cabbage
- 1 tablespoon chopped fresh cilantro leaves
- 2 tablespoons crushed salted tortilla chips

Meals in a Bag

Prepare any type of meal at home, (freeze if needed), and take in a heavy-duty freezer zip-tight plastic bag. When ready to eat, place the entire bag of food into a pot of boiling water to re-heat. The bag keeps the food dry while heating, and the water is gentler than direct flames from the campfire or camp stove.

Omelet

Mix the following in a heavy-duty freezer zip-tight plastic bag and keep cool with ice. When ready to eat, place bag in pot of boiling water until eggs are thoroughly cooked.

- Eggs, milk, cheese, salt, pepper (onion, vegetables, meat)

Pancakes

Mix the following in a heavy-duty freezer zip-tight plastic bag. When ready to eat, place bag in pot of boiling water until warm.

- Cooked pancakes, already covered in butter and syrup

See It Online: Shugemery is Inspirational in many ways

Heating Water

There are many ways to get hot water when camping—you may already have your favorite method. I have two favorites, since I often plan short trips where the only thing I need to heat is water—rather than cooking food directly over a stove or campfire.

- **Metal Water Bottle:** You can get these aluminum or steel bottles most anywhere for $10 to $20, but I pick up mine from the thrift store for about $1.00 for a large 16 to 20 ounce size bottle. Get one for each person on your trip. I make sure it has a water-tight cap (screwed on) to carry drinking water in my backpack, and some sort of ridge so I can lift it off of the campfire or stove when the water inside is boiling hot. After it cools, I keep it in a plastic bag so the soot on the outside doesn't make a mess of things inside my backpack.
- **Kelly Kettle:** This cooking system is amazing—especially for making hot water for tea, hot chocolate, coffee, soup, noodles, or a full dinner. There are three kit sizes (each in aluminum or stainless steel) and a number of accessories that can be added to each Kelly Kettle kit. They all work great. The one I use and recommend to get started is the Kelly Kettle Stainless Steel Medium Scout Basic Camp Stove Kit. There's also a YouTube video demonstrating how to use it.

Food: Easy Cooking

Remember that coals are hotter and more even in temperature compared to flames, which also add more smoke and soot to your food or cookware.

Basic Concepts

Cooking Temperature

Hold the back of your hand over the hot coals where you will be placing your food to cook. Measure the time you are able to withstand the heat before pulling your hand back.

- 1 to 2 seconds: High Heat - over 500 °F
- 4 to 5 seconds: Medium Heat - about 400 °F
- 7 to 9 seconds: Low Heat - about 300 °F
- 10 to 15 seconds: Very Low Heat - about 200 °F
- 20 to 30 seconds: Likely insufficient heat; add more fuel.

Cooking Methods

Plan ahead to be sure that you have the needed equipment to cook your food. For example, to boil water you must have some sort of pot, and frying will require a frying pan. With creativity, you can limit needed utensils to lightweight aluminum foil, well-placed rocks, or hand-crafted sticks.

- Baking in a Dutch Oven
- Baking in a reflective oven
- Baking in aluminum foil
- Boiling in a pot, sauce pan, tin can, etc.
- Cooking over campfire in pressure cooker – safe time & fuel
- Cooking over coals (or directly on coals)
- Frying on a pan or stone
- Roasting on a spit or sticks
- Roasting over flames

Roasting

In the context of campfire cooking, roasting is generally a method of holding food in close proximity to the dry heat of flames or coals (preferred) to warm or cook the food. The following are common examples of quick and easy items for roasting.

- Hot dogs
- Chicken nuggets
- Marshmallows
- Biscuits (bannock)
- Shish-ka-bobs

Roasted chicken nuggets on dinner rolls with mustard and cheese is my favorite.

Grilling

Grilling food over a bed of hot coals requires a grate of some sort, but little else. Here are some frequently used items for grilling.

- Hamburgers
- Chicken
- Steaks
- Fish
- Hot dogs
- Shish-ka-bobs
- Vegetables

Grilling is my favorite method for preparing vegetables.

Frying

Add a hot pan to the grill or hot coals and you can fry most anything in hot oil or butter. These are a few examples.

- Sausage
- Eggs
- Fish
- Potatoes
- Apple slices

My favorite is a thick steak placed directly on hot coals.

Pie Irons

These hinged plates on long sticks go by many names, including mountain pie makers, hobo pie irons, pudgy pie plates, and more. You can get them in sturdy cast iron, more lightweight cast aluminum, or even pressed aluminum. To use a pie iron, simply put most anything you like between two slices of buttered bread and heat in a campfire. You can also use them open like a frying pan. The options are limitless.

Sample Breakfast Recipe

- Pre-heat pie iron
- Two slices of hearty (whole grain) bread per sandwich
- Butter each slice (and/or spray cooking oil on the hot pie iron)
- Fill sandwich with cooked sausage, cheese, and an egg
- Cook for a couple of minutes on each side

NOTE: The length of time depends on campfire temperature

Popular Pie Iron Sandwiches

- **Grilled Cheese**
- **Ham & Cheese**
- **Turkey & Vegetables**
- **Tuna & Cheese**
- **Roast Beef:** with Swiss cheese, and mustard
- **Chipped Beef:** with BBQ sauce
- **Reuben:** with coleslaw
- **Philly Cheese Steak:** with grilled peppers, onions, mushrooms
- **Tampa Cuban:** pork, pickles, salami, cheese, and mustard
- **Rib Eye Steak Panini:** steak, arugula, peppers, and cheese
- **Pizza:** tomato sauce, cheese, pepperoni, and spices
- **Tacos:** cooked ground beef, cheese, tomato, spices
- **Sloppy Joes:** cooked ground beef in a BBQ sauce
- **Eggs & Sausage:** use pre-cooked sausage
- **Cherry Fruit Filling:** look for cans or jars
- **Apple Fruit Filling:** look for cans or jars
- **S'mores:** chocolate, marshmallow, and graham

Wrapped Baking

The following "wrapped cooking" concepts can be applied to use of a Dutch Oven, aluminum foil, large pots, or food wrapped in leaves—slowly baking in moderately hot coals (or on a grill) in a fire pit. Here are some basic ideas for recipes.

- **One-pot meals:** chili, beef stew, meatloaf, pizza, whole chicken, pork roast, meat & vegetable combo
- **Easy desserts:** baked apples, berry cobbler, coffee cake
- **Meat & potatoes:** combine ground meat, potato, carrot, catsup or BBQ sauce, onion, salt, and pepper. Bake for 10 minutes on each side.
- **Pizza pocket:** combine the following in a pita pocket—tomato sauce, cooked meat, cheese, onion, mushrooms, and spices. Bake for a 2 to 4 minutes on each side.
- **Leftovers burritos:** add any sort of leftovers from other meals to a tortilla (meats, cheeses, sauces, vegetables, seasonings, dessert toppings, or sandwich fillers), roll up, wrap in foil, bake until hot.

TIPS for cooking with aluminum foil

- Don't wrap too tightly. Leave room for steam inside of foil to help the food cook faster and more gently.
- When hot, cutting open with a knife or scissors may be easier than trying to unwrap it.
- To keep liquids from leaking out of wrapped foil—like for a family-sized beef & vegetable stew, secure a plastic oven bag inside the aluminum foil.
- Consider using a double layer of foil to minimize scorching and avoid leaking liquids.
- Much like a frying pan, try using butter or oil to keep things from sticking to the sides.
- Wrap in ice cubes to add water for moist steam.
- Assemble foil-wrapped meals before you go. Just take out of plastic bags and drop into the fire. No pots, no pans, no dishes, and virtually no cleanup.

- Using pre-cooked vegetables takes less time to heat up and may better balance other things in your foil pocket.
- To get crispier food (or less soggy), try poking small holes with a knife or fork to let the steam out during cooking.

Learn more by searching the Internet for "how-to" articles and demonstration videos.

Food: Harvesting Plants

When you are out in nature—especially in the summer, there is typically an abundance of plant life all around you. And much of it is not only edible, it is more nutritious than your candy bar or even your whole-grain, sugar-free, high-fiber breakfast bar! Learn to identify the edible plants in your area—or at least a few of them, so you can take advantage of healthy greens for a snack, to supplement your camp meals, or in case of emergency.

Inedible Plants

First, a warning. In addition to the many wild plants that are edible and tasty, some are quite poisonous. Learn to avoid these categorical plants, which cannot be eaten.

General Warning Signs

- Avoid plants that smell like almonds, which may have cyanide.
- Avoid plants with leaves in clusters of three (like poison ivy).
- Avoid plants with seeds inside a pod.
- Avoid plants with dill, carrot, parsnip, or parsley-like foliage.
- Avoid if it smells particularly strong or unpleasant.
- Avoid grain heads that are black, pink, or purple.
- Do not eat mushrooms—it's never worth the risk.
- Do not eat plants with sap that is milky or discolored.
- Do not eat plants that have shiny leaves.
- Do not eat plants that have thorns.
- Do not eat plants that have yellow or white berries.
- Do not eat plants that taste bitter or soapy.
- Do not eat umbrella-shaped flowers.

Plant Edibility Testing

Plant Parts

To better understand what plants are edible, first understand that different parts of a plant have different components that affect their edibility as well as their taste. So even though one part may be delicious, another part of the same plant may be highly poisonous. This is not only true of wild plants but those found in your grocery store as well. Remember these distinct plant parts.

- Roots
- Stems
- Leaves
- Buds (if available)
- Flowers (if available)

CAUTION: Only use this edibility test on plants that you are already reasonably confident are edible. Do NOT just pick any random plant and start testing; some plants are so poisonous that consuming even a small quantity could make you violently ill or even cause death. Please be careful.

General Observations

- See previous list, above, describing plants to avoid.
- Remove any worms or insects before testing for edibility.
- Avoid if you see many worms or parasites on the plant, as it is likely dead and rotting.

Prepare for Testing

- Test only one part of the plant at a time.
- Ideally, fast for several hours before testing anything.
- Do not eat anything else while testing.
- Be consistent in food preparation, like cooking time & method.

Sensitivity Testing

- **Skin Test:** Test the plant part on sensitive skin areas, like rubbing it inside elbow or wrist for a few minutes. Wait several hours; if you have no negative reaction, continue to the next step. (Bad signs include burning, itching, bumps, welts, or redness.)

- **Prepare:** Since some toxic plants become edible after cooked or boiled, consider preparing the plant part as you typically would for eating. For example, boiling leaves like spinach.
- **Lips Test:** Rub the plant part across your moist lips. If no negative reaction, no bitter or soapy taste, and no burning sensation, continue to the next step.
- **Gums Test:** Place a very small piece of the plant part in your mouth between your lower lip and gum for several minutes (do not swallow). If no burning or tingling, continue to the next step.
- **Tongue Test:** Place the same very small piece of the plant part in your mouth and hold it on your tongue for another 15 minutes (do not swallow any). If you do not experience anything unpleasant, continue to the next step. (It may not taste great, but taste alone does not indicate edibility.)
- **Chew Test:** After holding the plant part on your tongue for 15 minutes, chew it thoroughly and wait another 15 minutes without swallowing. If nothing negative—no burning, no numbness, no tingling, then continue to the next step.
- **Swallow Test:** Now that you've had this soggy mess in your mouth for half an hour, go ahead a swallow it and wait for several hours. Give you stomach time to communicate with you about any sort of negative reactions. If you feel nauseous, try to vomit and drink plenty of water. If you feel fine, continue to the next step. While you wait, you could read a good book—like this one!
- **Eating Test:** Collect and eat a single serving (a small handful) of the exact same part of the plant that you tested... and wait for several hours to give your body time to react. Also, avoid eating anything else while you are waiting. During this time, you could go fishing, hunting, or gather firewood.
- **Enjoy:** If all is well at this point, then this part of this plant should be fine to eat. Remember that other parts of the same plant will still need the same sensitivity testing.

Edible Plants

Become very familiar with edible plants before eating them.

- Receive first-hand training from an experienced person
- Watch online videos that make plant identification easy
- Read books that are very detailed in plant descriptions

Berries, Fruits, & Nuts

- **Wild Berries:** Blackberries, black caps, blueberries, chokeberries, cloudberries, cranberries, dewberries, elderberries, gooseberries, huckleberries, mulberries, muscadine, raspberries, serviceberries (juneberries), wild cherries, wild strawberries, and wild grapes. These are just the basics; there are dozens more in your region.

Avoid all white or yellow berries.

- **Feral Fruit Trees:** Apple, apricot, cherry, citrus, crabapple, paw paw, peach, pear, plum

Avoid trees with small clusters of berry-sized fruit

- **Tree Nuts:** Acorns, hazelnuts, hickory nuts, walnuts

Greens

Consider reviewing Pinterest edible plants images or a YouTube video like 36 Wild Edibles to review plants that you already recognize. This may include common plants like Dandelion, Raspberry, Mint, Plantain, Garlic Mustard, Chickweed, Boneset, Trilliums, Violets, Black Eyed Susan, Wild Carrot (Queen Anne's Lace), Clover, Yarrow, Jewelweed, and more.

The following plants are usually easy to find and easy to identify.

- **Cattails:** Found near marshy ponds, cattails are almost entirely edible. Roots can be cooked like potatoes. Stems and leaves can also be eaten raw or cooked. See the **Tools: Cattails** > Food section in Chapter 5 for more information.
- **Chickweed:** Found in most Easter U.S. woodlands, chickweed is both nutritious and tasty. Learn to identify chickweed online. Look for clusters of smooth leaves and make sure there are no red

spots on the leaf underside (indicating a poisonous look-alike plant).

- **Clover:** Flowers and leaves of clover can be eaten raw or boiled.
- **Dandelion:** The yellow flower and green leaves of dandelion are often used in gourmet salads. The roots are also quite nutritious. Leaves may be boiled or eaten raw. The roots are best roasted or boiled.
- **Fiddlehead Ferns:** Remove the brown scales and cook as you would cook green beans.
- **Lamb's Quarters:** Eat both the leaves and seeds of Lamb's Quarters or "Wild Spinach," raw or cooked (preferred). For identification, look for waxy, white crystals that can be rubbed off of the broad leaves and ribbed stem. Plants can be several feet tall and each branch node may have a purple mark.
- **Lilac:** Enjoy the sweet lemon flavor when blooming in the spring.
- **Plantain:** The round, green leaves of plantain are great raw or cooked, much like spinach. The younger, smaller, lighter colored leaves are more tender and tasty. The seeds can be dried and ground for a flour substitute in pancakes and breads or to thicken soups. The thick veins in this plain can also be used like cording to tie things together.
- **Thistle:** Skip the spiky parts with the purple flowers, and go for the thistle stems, chopped and cooked.
- **Trillium:** Enjoy eating the leaves of trillium, raw or cooked.
- **Other Wild Edibles** that you may already recognize include: amaranth, acorns, bull thistle, chives, curly dock, elder flower, field mustard, fireweed, hibiscus, mallow, pine cone seeds, pigweed, pine needles, sheep sorrel, stinging nettles, sunflower, watercress, wild asparagus, wild mustard, wild onions, wild violets, and wood sorrel.

See More Online: Wild Edibles Identification - YouTube Videos

Get a good edible plants book at Amazon.com

Foraged Teas

Steep these plants in hot water for a delightful hot tea drink in the wild. While the leaves are usually steeped, you may also use flowers, roots, berries, or combinations for optimal taste or medicinal value. Many of these teas will taste better with a bit of sweetener.

Be 100% certain of plant identification before using for tea!

- **Acorn and Oak Bark *:** high tannic acid
- **Birch Sap *:** nutritious
- **Birch Twigs (Black or Yellow Birch):** wintergreen flavor
  > Small handful of cut twigs, steep 20 to 30 minutes, sweeten
- **Blackberry Leaf *:** high in vitamin C, high tannic acid
- **Blueberry Leaf:** nutritious
  > Bake leaves at 400 for 30 min, grind to powder, steep 3 minutes
- **Chamomile (all varieties) *:** immune system booster
- **Cleavers (goosegrass, stickywilly, catchweed):** springtime
- **Cowslip Flowers *:** steep 10 minutes
- **Dandelion *:** flower, leaf, or root
- **Elderberry & Elderflower *:** use flowers or fruits only
- **Lavender Flowers *:** rub on skin for a bug repellent
- **Lemon Balm *:** many medicinal properties
- **Mallow *:** nutritious
- **Milk Thistle *:** flower, leaf, or root
- **Mint *:** nutritious, decongestant
- **Mullein (Verbascum thapsus) *:** immune system booster
- **Nettle (Stinging Nettle):** roast over flame to remove needles
  > Use gloves to avoid being stung by needles
- **Pinapple Weed (like Chamomile):** tasty
- **Pine, Spruce, or Conifer Needle *:** high vitamin C
  > Use green needles, trim off brown ends, steep 5 to 10 minutes
- **Plantain *:** nutritious
- **Raspberry Leaf:** nutritious
- **Red Clover:** avoid if pregnant
  > Gather a handful of red/pink blossoms, steep 10 minutes
- **Rose:** fragrant
- **Rosehip *:** immune system booster

- **Sassafras Roots:** avoid if pregnant
  > Wash, cut, dry, peel bark, boil 20 minutes, add sweetener
- **Spicebush:** use dried twigs with berries in winter
- **Wild Ginger:** use root
- **Willow Bark *:** somewhat like Aspirin
- **Yarrow:** delicious

** These flagged teas have medicinal purposes also*

Food: Harvesting Animals

When you are hungry in the woods, you might first think of vegetation like fruits and greens, or you might think of meats for protein and fat. If you hunger for protein, then harvesting fresh meat may be very rewarding for you. Of course, check to be sure that hunting game and harvesting protected animals is legal and in season for your location.

Near the Water

Fishing

Fish: Confirm seasons for each species

- Consider angling, netting, spearing, trapping, or noodling
- Use fish guts as bait to catch more fish or larger fish

Frogs: Requires a fishing license in many U.S. states

- Consider a net, a spear gig, or a fish hook with red yarn
- Use frog guts as bait to catch fish

Remember that hunting and fishing require either a valid sporting license & corresponding seasons, or a life-or-death survival situation.

Trapping & Gathering

A variety of shellfish are often available—not only along the seashore, but also along many freshwater waterways. If you are new to eating foraged shellfish, avoid late spring and summer to prevent possible toxic poisoning.

- **Shorelines:** Mussels, scallops, oysters, cockles, winkles, whelks
- **Various Locations:** Crayfish, crabs, shrimp, clams, turtles

In the Field

The key to harvesting wild animals is the tools you currently have available. Do you have weapons, traps, snares, or the skills and materials needed to create these?

Trapping and snaring might only be legal if needed for survival.

Small Animals

- **Game:** rabbit, hare, squirrel, prairie dog, opossum, snake
- **Non-Game:** turtle, gopher, beaver, martin, mink, weasel, otter
- **Survival:** coyote, fox, musk rat, raccoon, porcupine, armadillo, mice, chipmunk, packrat, mole, woodchuck
- **Birds:** turkey, pheasant, quail, grouse, partridge, woodcock, dove, ducks, geese, waterfowl, crow, songbirds

The quality of the meat you harvest may depend on how hungry you are.

Consider the following methods or devices for harvesting small animals. Some are only allowed when used for survival.

- **Firearms:** Rifle, shotgun, handgun, air rifle
- **Slings:** Archery, slingshot, Bushcraft nun chucks (two rocks tied together by two feet of cording)
- **Traps:** Cable snares, box traps, nets, Conibear
- **Baiting:** Food, lures, scents, decoys
- **Calling or Driving** into a key location, like a trap or killing zone
- **Spotlighting** at night to locate and target dazed animals
- **Tracking**, scouting, glassing, and stalking
- **Research:** Consider reading about how to make your own traps

Quick Set: Tether and set 25-cent mouse traps and bait with birdseed. Good for birds, squirrel, mice, moles, and more.

Near the Ground

Eating insects and tiny animals may seem gross, but you don't need any permission or license to harvest loads of insects and they can be a great source of nutrition and energy. Remember that in many countries outside the United States, eating arthropods is common as a main dish or side dishes with everyday meals—not just for survival. Common insect flavors include nutty, buttery, and "like chicken."

Most bugs are fine to eat, but here are some cautions to remember.

- **Avoid** insects that bite or sting
- **Avoid** insects with bright colors, especially red, orange, yellow
- **Avoid** bugs with hairy or furry bodies

- **Avoid** disease-carrying bugs like mosquitoes, flies, or ticks
- **Avoid** insects in urban areas where pesticides may be used
- **Avoid** insects that smell foul, or are found near foul-smelling carcasses—except for maggots, which are fine to eat

Here are the basics for eating insects.

- **Look** under fallen logs and dig through rotting wood
- **Look** in tall, grassy fields
- **Remove wings and legs** before eating or cooking
- **Heads** may also be pulled off, often taking guts with them
- **Cook** whenever possible to kill any possible parasites—roast, fry, or boil for 2 to 5 minutes
- **Season** with salt (and pepper or other spices)
- **Grind** cooked bugs into a powder or paste and mix with salad greens, soup, or tea—so you don't feel like you are eating bugs
- **Fat White Grubs** found under rotting logs can be eaten raw

Try grilled grasshoppers with salt, chili powder, and lime for a crunchy snack.

Insects to look for include the following.

- **Near Grass:** Crickets, grasshoppers, cicadas, locusts
- **Near Wood:** Larvae, grubs, ants, termites, beetles, cockroaches

Packed with calories, a black soldier fly larvae is 35% fat and 42% protein.

Consider the following harvesting methods for these tiny animals.

- **Easy:** Use your fingers and a small container—like your hand
- **Morning:** Insects like grasshoppers are slower in cool mornings
- **Flying/Jumping:** Netting or a handkerchief or shirt attached to two long sticks
- **Ants:** Poke a stick into an ant hill; when they climb it, shake into a container
- **Swatter:** A sapling tree branch—like a fly swatter, to stun hoppers and pick them up before they move again
- **Traps:** Various traps like a baited jar left overnight
- **Dig:** Use a heavy stick to dig into soft dirt under fallen trees

Food: Chapter Review

Chapter Summary

Remember these categories of food preparation for your next trip.

- **Basic Preparation:** Condiments, drinks, medicine, safety
- **No Cooking:** Meats, vegetables, starches, sweets, drinks
- **Just Add Hot Water:** Drinks, meals in a cup, meals in a bag
- **Easy Cooking:** Basics, roasting, grilling, frying, pie irons, wraps
- **Harvesting Plants:** Inedible plants, identifying edible plants
- **Harvesting Animals:** Near water, in the field, or on the ground

Chapter Action Steps

☐ Think of which of these food preps you can do now and have your backpack or cooler already set to go on your next trip.

☐ Try some of these recipes at home to see what combination of ingredients works best for you.

☐ Go ahead and freeze or freeze-dry some meals so they are ready to go.

☐ Create a menu or food shopping list for your next outing.

☐ Do some research online or in books to improve your skills at identifying edible and tasty plants in the wild.

☐ Purchase some edible insects to cook and eat at home—prove to yourself that you can do it!

I don't need therapy. I just need to go camping! ☺

Next Chapter

Now that you're ready to start a fire, you have plenty of drinkable water, and your food planning is complete, let's invest some time in where to camp and how to prepare your shelter.

Chapter 4. Shelter

Shelter: Chapter Intro

If you're going to be outdoors for any length of time—or overnight, you will likely need some sort of protection to keep warm and dry. This chapter on shelter includes the following topics.

Shelter: Campsite Location

When selecting an ideal backcountry location to make camp and set up shelter, there are several factors to consider. Remember that no site will be perfect, so balance your personal priorities with safety, convenience, and what is available.

- **Timing:** Plan to arrive at your campsite location with one or two hours of daylight for shelter setup, firewood collection, etc.
- **Water Access:** If you will need water for drinking, cooking, and washing, camp within a short distance of fresh water.
- **Waterline:** Whether you are near a lake, stream, beach, river, or other body of water, be sure to stay above the waterline—even if it doesn't rain where you are, rainfall upstream in the mountains may come gushing down on you while you are sleeping. Many parks require that you be at least 200 feet away from any running water to avoid being caught in a flash flood.
- **Water Drainage:** If it might rain while you are camped, be sure to avoid pitching a tent or building a fire in small valleys or drainage basins that will retain rain water.
- **Firewood:** Look around to ensure that sufficient amount of quality firewood is available within a short walking distance.
- **Bushcraft:** If you plan to build anything like a shelter frame, ridgeline, bench, rake, or gadgets—identify suitable materials.
- **Minimize Impact:** Avoid trampling a pristine meadow, damaging vegetation, or spoiling scenery for others. If you are in a large group, consider dividing into smaller sites.

Some campsites are closed due to site abuse. Many parks are completely closed to any type of camping because of carelessness. Please leave it as you found it.

- **Pests:** Avoid areas that have nearby wasp nests; bee hives; ant hills; stagnant water breeding mosquitos; tall grass harboring mice, ticks, chiggers, and ants; deadfalls or rocky terrain that may be home to snakes; or nearby caves that might have bears.
- **Plants:** Avoid camping around poison ivy, poison oak, nettles, or similar plants to which you may have an allergic reaction.

- **Overhead Hazards:** Do not camp near dead trees or tree limbs that are still hanging above ground, beneath cliffs with loose rocks that may fall, or anything else that may fall with wind in the night. These are called widow makers.
- **Surface:** If tenting, you will need a flat, level surface at least the size of your tent floor for comfortable sleeping. Avoid bumps, slopes, or uneven ground. If you are using a hammock, this is far less important. Remember to clear away any fire hazards.
- **Wind Block:** To avoid a bitter cold breeze, camp next to a natural wind barrier like dense trees, large rocks, or thick brush.
- **Breeze:** A clearing in the woods or on a hillside that encourages a warm breeze may help keep away bugs, bees, and mosquitos.
- **Bear Bag:** Keep animals out of your food by camping where you can hang your food in a bear bag 100 yards downwind.

"Bear bells can be an effective method to avoid confrontation with a startled bear. The challenge is getting the bells to stay on the bear." ☺

- **Buffer Zone:** Keep at least 200 feet away from any hiking trails, rivers, streams, lakes, or other campsites. Also avoid game trails to minimize animals bumping into you during the night.
- **Avoid Overcrowding:** Do your best to not camp too close to others, spoiling their view, being noisy, or limiting trail access.
- **Waste Management:** Plan ahead for where (and how) to "go to the bathroom" to avoid contamination or embarrassment.
- **Land Usage:** Remember to respect private property and any park rules for your type of camping.
- **Hunting Seasons:** Remember to make yourself visible during any local hunting seasons, typically with bright orange.
- **Bearings:** When circling around and settling into your site, be sure that you remember how to return to where you came from.
- **Communication:** Do you need cell phone reception in case of emergency? A nearby hilltop may help pick up a cell signal.

MORE: Did I forget any good tips on campsite selection? Send them to me at PrepListsBooks.com > Feedback, where it may be included in the Resources web page, or part of a future book. Thanks!

Shelter: Sleeping

When camping, where you sleep depends on so many conditions, like temperature, weather, terrain, resources at hand, and more. Here are some basics to consider for your planning.

Tents

Whether you are purchasing a tent or building a make-shift tent-line shelter, these construction and design elements can be useful.

Tent Type Selection

Selecting the best tent for your needs can be quite a challenge. Consider the following to help in your decision-making process.

Ridge Tent: classic triangle with cross-pole

- PROS: Stable, quick and easy, best for sleeping only
- CONS: Low height, small space for moving around
- TIPS: Build yourself with a branch and a tarp or rain poncho

See Resources chapter for pictures, styles, pricing, and reviews for ridge tents

Dome (Umbrella) Tent: flexible poles in a hemisphere

- PROS: Stable, quick and easy, lightweight, more room
- CONS: Large ones less stable in wind & more difficult to set up
- TIPS: Build yourself by tying saplings together

See Resources chapter for pictures, styles, pricing, and reviews for dome tents

Frame Tent: rigid poles

- PROS: Sturdy, large
- CONS: Heavy, bulky, more difficult to set up
- TIPS: Bring your truck

See Resources chapter for pictures, styles, pricing, and reviews for frame tents

Quick-Pitch or Instant Tent: spring-loaded or coiled frame

- PROS: Quick and easy
- CONS: Often more of a toy than a serious camping tent
- TIPS: Avoid in rough weather. Consider for keeping gear dry.

See Resources chapter for pictures, styles, pricing, and reviews for quick-pitch tents

Geodesic and Semi-Geodesic Tent: criss-cross poles

- PROS: Very sturdy in harsh, windy conditions
- CONS: Expensive
- TIPS: Probably overkill for most leisurely camping

See Resources chapter for pictures, styles, pricing, and reviews for geodesic tents

Inflatable Tent: compressed air

- PROS: Fun to set up
- CONS: Heavy and bulky, requires air compressor
- TIPS: Use next to your truck or car

See Resources chapter for pictures, styles, pricing, and reviews for inflatable tents

Family or Cabin Tent: huge, multiple rooms

- PROS: Large size for lots of people and lots of gear
- CONS: More expensive, sometimes unreliable
- TIPS: Coordinate smaller tents to meet under a canopy

See Resources chapter for pictures, styles, pricing, and reviews for family cabin tents

Tunnel Tent: dome tents side-by-side

- PROS: Expandable for families or groups
- CONS: Limited applications, heavy and bulky
- TIPS: Often more functional than family tents

See Resources chapter for pictures, styles, pricing, and reviews for tunnel tents

Pod Tent: arranged like spokes around central living space

- PROS: Great for separation and compartmentalization
- CONS: Requires large, flat ground surface
- TIPS: Consider a set up using only some of the pods

See Resources chapter for pictures, styles, pricing, and reviews for pod tents

Tent Pitching Prep

Remember these tips before pitching or setting up your tent.

If it's been a while since you used the tent, set it up at home first

- Make sure you have all the pieces and all stakes
- Make sure it does not have mold or mildew
- Make sure you remember how to set it up (in daylight)
- Make sure there is no damage that needs repair
- Consider a fresh coat of rain-proofing spray

Before you go, decide what to take

- Determine if you need a groundsheet under or inside it
- Decide if you need a sleeping pad, air mattress, or other support
- Consider a door mat or throw rug for wiping wet shoes, collecting dirt, comfort, warmth, etc.
- Consider reducing your pack weight by changing or eliminating something like metal stakes or a rainfly. Maybe all you need is the rainfly.
- Depending on tent condition and length of trip, would a tent repair kit (or silicone spray) be wise to take with you?

Before pitching the tent

- Note of how the tent is packed (cell phone photos?) so that you can return it to this condition when it's time to pack up again.
- Select position and door direction: relative to campfire, the wind, the trail, the sun, or desired privacy.
- Clear the area of all rocks, sticks, acorns, etc. to avoid a lumpy bed. Build and use a rake to make this easier.
- Consider piling extra leaves or grass under the tent like a mattress for extra comfort and warmth. Build and use a rake to make this easier.

Tent Takedown Planning

Consider the following when taking down your tent.

- Use a whisk broom or towel to clean out all dirt, leaves, etc.
- Make a note of any repairs needed for when you get home.
- Get the tent as dry as possible. If it is damp when packed out, remember to set it up at home to air out as soon as possible.
- Consider rolling up rain fly and ground tarp together with tent.
- Consider rolling tent around the poles to wrap more tightly.

Did you hear about the Native American Indian who told the psychiatrist, "I can't decide! I'm a wigwam, I'm a teepee, I'm a wigwam, I'm a teepee." The psychiatrist calmly replied, "Just relax. You're too tense!" (Two tents! Ha Ha!)

Ground

Sleeping on the ground can take many forms. From the simplest laying on the grass under the stars, to building a make-shift shelter out of nearby vegetation, or using a Bivy bag to keep rain off, sleeping on the ground can be made comfortable, warm, and dry.

A sleeping pad (or platform) is a layer of protection under you when sleeping—adding warmth, dryness, or comfort. It can be used by itself or combined with a sleeping bag, hammock, or tent.

Packed

Consider packing one of these sleeping platform ideas to go under your sleeping bag or blankets.

- **Foam Pad:** rolls up tightly for packing
- **Self-Inflating Pad:** draws in air when unrolled
- **Air Pad:** inflate yourself
- **Air Mattress:** inflate with a pump
- **Cot:** purchased or home-made
- **Extra Blankets:** or an old bedspread comforter

Some insulated sleeping pads can be inserted into your sleeping bag with straps or sleeves to avoid rolling off of it during the night.

Improvised

Improvise a mattress by covering any of the following with a tarp, blanket, coat, rain poncho, etc.

- **Pile of Leaves:** easier with a Bushcraft rake
- **Bed of Pine Needles:** under or next to a grove of evergreens
- **Long Grass:** cut or standing
- **Clothing:** stacked and spread out
- **Visor:** Reflective Car Sun Visor: also sitting or changing clothes
- **Cot with blanket:** build in the woods by lashing branches
- **Packed and formed snow:** shape to your body
- **Bedroll:** wrap blankets and padding inside a tarp

Sleeping Bag

When buying (or borrowing) a sleeping bag, consider these options and features to be best prepared.

Categories

- **Three-Season:** for temperatures **above 15** degrees
  > Moderate weight and size; may include extra warmth features
- **Winter:** for temperatures **below 15** degrees
  > Heavier and larger, complete with hoods, draft collars, foot box, pad sleeves or straps, baffling, stash pocket, etc.
- **Summer:** for temperatures **above 32** degrees
  > Lighter, smaller, easier, limited features

For warm nights, consider lightweight sheets or blankets instead of a heavy sleeping bag.

Features

- **Temperature** Ratings: helpful, but limited standardization
- **Shell**: Waterproof (more expensive) or not (typical)
- **Shape**: Rectangle (roomy and inexpensive), semi-rectangle (allowing some movement), mummy (max warmth and min size)
- **Insulation**: Down (best quality), synthetic (often best value, especially if it might get wet), or a combination

Remember to store your sleeping bag either open and hanging or in a larger bag, rather than compressed into a stuff sack. This will improve the insulation value by keeping the filling lofted.

Bags lose loft with use, so launder sleeping bags after 30 nights of use.

- **Weight**: Balance your personal needs between low weight or size (for backpacking), and roominess or comfort (for quality sleep)
- **Try before You Buy**: Get in, move around, cinch it up, use the zipper, consider any additions like a liner or pad to go inside

More expert advice about sleeping bags is available at the REI website.

Pillows

Don't underestimate the value of a good headrest while you are sleeping—especially for long trips. Consider these alternatives to the standard pillow that you use at home every night.

See It Online: Camping Pillows

- Camp pillow: inflated, stuffed, etc.
- Travel pillow
- Inflatable pillow
- Inflatable headrest (like those used on airplanes)
- Large zip-tight plastic bag (or multiple bags) in a cloth sack or wrapped in a T-Shirt
- Roll any of these into a log or stuff into a sack or plastic bag
  > Sweatshirt
  > T-Shirts
  > Towels
  > Blankets
- Fill trash bag with these and stuff in a sleeping bag sack or shirt
  > Leaves
  > Grass
  > Sand
  > Dirt

Hammocks

Using a hammock is a favorite of mine for the following reasons.

- More comfortable sleep
- Lightweight for backpacking
- Easier to find a suitable campsite in rocky or hilly terrain
- Multi-functional for camp seating
- Usually warmer than in a tent
- More versatile for different weather and activities

See It Online: Trek Light Gear - Hammock Camping 101:
5 Reasons Why You Should Switch from a Tent to a Hammock

Hammock gear depends mostly on temperature and precipitation.

If it's a warm, dry night then all you need is the hammock itself—rolled up into a jacket pocket or fanny pack.

If you need to escape from bugs or mosquitos, use a hammock with a screen—it zips up like a suspended tent.

If you expect rain, pack a rain fly or small tarp.

If it will be cold, consider a mix & match of the following.

- Hammock: with straps
- Sleeping bag: over quilt
- Fleece liner or flannel sheet: inside sleeping bag
- Car shade visor pad: under sleeping bag (doubles as seat pad and changing mat)
- Small utility bag: clipped inside hammock (with pillow, extra clothing, gloves, and head gear—like knit hat, balaclava, neck gaiter, hood, etc.)
- Under Quilt (or sleeping bag): attach to hammock straps
- Under Wrap (emergency Mylar blanket): attach cinched ends to carabiners on hammock straps
- Tarp rain fly, stakes, ridge poles, strapping, cording, sticks

See It Online: Shugemery - Hammock Hangin' How-To Videos

This is a winter hammock quick reference for SETUP SEQUENCE.

First, attach hammock and ridge pole to trees—using nylon straps at 6 to 7 feet above the ground

Next, set up each of the following OPTIONAL components:

- Attach lower ridge paracord in carabiners at 4 to 5 feet high
- Attach bug netting to lower ridge
- Cinch under quilt and attach to lower ridge
- Cinch under wrap and attach to carabiners
- Insert reflective car sun shade visor pad for extra warmth
- Insert sleeping bag or over quilt
- Insert fleece blanket or flannel sheet for extra warmth or a lighter sleeping bag
- Attach utility or ditty bag inside hammock for quick access
- Set up rain fly or rain tarp using the upper ridge pole

See Photos Online: Waterproof Hammock Rain Fly for Camping

See Setup Diagram Online: Hammock Under Quilt

See Photos Online: Hammock & Mosquito Net

Sleeping Accessories

Consider the following for greatest comfort and warmth while sleeping.

- Pillow or Headrest
- Ear Plugs
- Water Bottle
- Urine Bottle/Bag
- Flashlight
- Bug repellent

Do you like cool technology?
Check out this laser perimeter warning device that will set off an alarm if anyone or anything comes into your camping space. Bear beware!

Sleeping Warm

Often the biggest challenge for sleeping outdoors is keeping warm. Think about a combination of these options to stay comfortable on a chilly night.

Key Principles

- Insulate yourself to retain heat
- Keep as dry as possible

Head & Neck

- Knit hat – or any hat, lid, hood, stocking cap, or head covering
- Make-shift hat made from a handkerchief, shirt, bag, or towel
- Hooded sweatshirt – with hood cinched closed
- Scarf around your neck
- Balaclava – versatile for fine-tuning adjustments

In the Bag

- Change into clean, dry clothes (and underwear) when you get into bed to avoid moisture and improve insulation value
- Wear gloves, mittens, or anything wrapped around hands
- Wear long underwear and fresh, dry socks
- Wear loose-fitting clothing for air pockets and better circulation
- Wrap your feet in a sweatshirt to keep them warm and dry
- Fluff up your sleeping bag as soon as you arrive to improve the loft and insulation value OR keep sleeping bag rolled up until bedtime, to avoid getting damp DEPENDING on humidity
- Any sort of insulating barrier between you and the cold ground
- Stuff dry clothing into your sleeping bag for extra insulation
- Use layers of insulation to control moisture and avoid frost
- Breathe outside of sleeping bag to prevent dampness inside
- If too hot, allow bag to air out to avoid sweaty dampness
- Consider a "sleeping suit" of dry clothing kept in sleeping bag
- Allow sleeping bag to fully dry in the morning before rolling up—turn inside out and drape over tent to dry quickly

If it's zero degrees outside today and it's supposed to be twice as cold tomorrow, how cold is it going to be?

Bedtime Preparation

- Consider a sleeping bag that is rated for lower temperatures
- Launder sleeping bag to fluff it up and improve insulation value
- Use a flannel sheet or fleece blanket inside your sleeping bag
- Wrap your sleeping bag in a Mylar emergency blanket
- Eat a big meal before bed – for calories and warmth of digestion
- Take a candy bar to bed with you and eat if you wake up cold
- Drink a hot beverage before climbing into bed
- Drink up during the day, then stop an hour before bedtime—to avoid needing to get out of bed to urinate before morning.
- Do a minute of exercise to warm up before going to sleep
- Avoid getting into bed damp, sweaty, or warm enough to sweat
- Choose a campsite that is out of the wind and above the valley floor, where cold air settles overnight
- Heat dry rocks in campfire, then place under your sleeping area
- Add warm water to a water bottle and hold against your core
- Have a snack ready to eat if you wake in the middle of the night
- Use your backpack or a zipped-up coat as a foot cover for extra insulation while sleeping
- A safely-hung candle lantern in your tent provides warmth and reduces condensation.

CAUTION: If bear may be nearby, do not keep food, empty food wrappers, or anything that smells like food in your sleeping area.

Staying Warm

- Use a pee bottle to urinate during the night, rather than going out into the cold
- If your sleeping bag has a drawstring, pull it around your face, not around your neck, keeping your mouth and nose exposed
- Eat a midnight snack if you wake cold—something calorie dense
- Consider a safe campfire design that produces long-term heat
- Snuggle up or spoon with someone to share body heat
- Sleep in the fetal position, curled up to better retain core heat
- Keep your next day's footwear (and clothing) in a plastic bag and place in your sleeping bag to warm up

Sleeping Cool

Getting a good night's sleep is a challenge when the heat is too much to get comfortable. Consider these ideas to stay cool outdoors.

Bedding

- Instead of a winter sleeping bag, use a lightweight one
- Instead of a sleeping bag, just use sheets or a light blanket

Clothing

- Wear loose, breathable clothing; minimize clothes to vent heat
- Soak bandana, hat, sock, etc. with cool water and place on head or feet
- Start sleep with cool water bottles

Location

- Position tent or rainfly so that breezes enter or pass through
- Look for a shady and breezy campsite to minimize the heat

Remember that if you are exposing yourself to wind to stay cool, it will pull moisture out of you, so stay well-hydrated by drinking plenty of water.

- When seeking shade, note the direction the sun is moving
- Use large tarp to create a shaded area and block sun's heat
- Air around and above a moving stream will be cooler

Bedtime Preparation

- Drape a reflective blanket over tent to minimize heat from sun
- Use a reflective blanket or tarp under bedding if ground is hot
- Open tent windows to encourage movement of air
- Consider changing from a tent to a hammock with rainfly
- Stay well-hydrated by drinking plenty of water during the day
- Take an inflatable kiddie pool for you, kids, or pets to play in
- Before bed, remove boots or wear sandals to help cool down
- Wading in a nearby stream or lake will cool your whole body

Shelter: Weather

Proper gear, clothing, and shelter for the ever-changing weather is key to enjoying every moment of your adventure. Will it be cold, hot, wet, dry, snowy, foggy, dark, or all of the above?

For more information on these weather-related topics, please see the **Skills: Weather Preparation** section in Chapter 6.

Shelter: Chapter Review

Chapter Summary

Remember these shelter topics to maximize your camping comfort.

- Selecting the best **campsite location** is key to enjoying everything else on your camping trip
- Your **sleeping plans** may include various combinations of tents, sleeping bags, pillows, hammocks, and other accessories for the best sleep you can get away from home
- There are many low-tech methods to **sleep warm** on a cold night or to **stay cool** on a hot night
- Always be prepared for **changes in weather**, including rain, snow, cold, heat, or even darkness

Chapter Action Steps

☐ Be sure your tent and sleeping gear are always ready to go.

☐ Set up your tent in the backyard to be sure you have all parts and remember how to do it quickly, even in rain or in the dark.

☐ Consider upgrading your sleeping gear for improved comfort, more warmth, less weight, smaller size, or flexibility.

☐ Try out the various methods for managing uncomfortable temperatures to see what works best for you.

☐ Review the various equipment and resources available to order online before your next trip.

Camping: Spending a small fortune to live like a homeless person. ☺

Next Chapter

In the last four chapters, we've covered fire, water, food, and shelter. Now let's look at how to make the most of the tools you have with you. You'll be amazed at how you can improvise everyday items.

Chapter 5. Tools

Tools: Chapter Intro

When planning for the unexpected, remember that redundancy (multiple ways to accomplish the same task) and multiple-use items (utilization) can be the difference between fun and frantic.

This chapter alone—about improvising with everyday items, is worth the price of this book! Read it once for future brainstorming when you're in a pinch. Read it again for better memory retention. Take it with you for optimal value.

This chapter on tools includes the following topics.

Tools: Mylar Blanket

These compact and lightweight blankets are known by various names: Mylar, emergency, rescue, reflective, tinfoil, space, or thermal blankets. Made from a thin sheet of plastic or film and coated with a metallic reflecting agent—usually silver, orange, or gold, these inexpensive tools have many uses and utilizations.

Compare Mylar Prices: Emergency Blanket Options

Capabilities & Principles

Reflects Heat

- Keep warm (absorb heat from sun or fire)
- Keep cool (block heat from sun)

Windproof

- Collect wind (dry off, air out, harness energy)
- Contain smoke to preserve meat
- Keep wind out

Lightproof

- Camouflage
- Shade from sun
- Reflect sunlight for signaling, heating, or cooking

Waterproof

- Collect water (from rain, stream, or vapor)
- Keep water out (rain fly, ground sheet, wrap around clothing or electronics)

Airtight

- Reduce perspiration evaporation for warmth
- Stop convection flow to keep warm
- Wrap food to protect it
- Contain smoke to preserve meat

See It Online: Heavy Duty Survival Blanket

Applications

- **Combine Multiple Blankets:** Tie together for larger areas
- **Cooking Or Baking:** Line a container with the blanket to create a solar oven, reflecting sunlight into a central point
- **Cordage:** Cut the Mylar into thin strips and braid together for added strength
- **Disinfect Drinking Water:** Much like a solar oven, use to heat water to a boil, or position behind water bottles to speed up the process of ultraviolet radiation from the sun to disinfect water.
- **Dry Clothing Faster:** Spread clothes out on Mylar and place in the sunlight, turning frequently to dry out more quickly
- **Fire Starter:** Create a concave parabolic mirror to concentrate sunlight into a tiny spot that heats into a flame.
- **First Aid:** Cut into strips to make immobilizing sling or splints
- **Fishing Lures:** Wrap pieces of the shiny metal around a hook to look like a swimming minnow
- **Ground Sheet:** Lay under tent, sleeping bag, or yourself to keep moisture from the ground off of you.
- **Hammock Underquilt:** Forget the heavy, bulky wraps, try this lightweight alternative to staying warm in your hammock
- **Heat Reflector:** Hang reflector on opposite side of campfire to redirect radiant heat toward you and your sleeping area
- **Heat Reflector:** To stay warm while sitting next to fire, hold the blanket (shiny side facing the flame) up above your head to create a pocket.
- **Heat Reflector:** To stay warm while sleeping, line the ceiling of A-frame shelter or lean-to next to any heat source to reflect radiating heat (including your own body heat) back toward you.
- **Hypothermia:** Retain body heat by huddling close to the ground with blanket loosely wrapped around and over... while building fire.
- **Poncho:** Wrap in Mylar blanket to keep warm and protect you and your gear from rain or snow
- **Preserve Meat:** Use large branches to build a tripod smoker frame with a triangular platform lashed in the middle, where you

will hang your meat. Cover the tripod with the blanket, leaving enough space at the bottom to tend a small fire. Limit airflow to keep the hardwood just smoldering for a smoky chamber. Smoked meat lasts a week.

- **Shelter Room:** String up like a tarp (using a stone and loop of cordage in each corner) to protect from rain and wind
- **Signal Passively:** Cut or tear the space blanket into small strips and tie them onto tree branches. These will sparkle in sunlight or from the beam of a flashlight and help rescuers find you.
- **Signal:** Reflect the sun with the shiny side to signal a distant observer or aircraft. Shake the blanket as if you're shaking dust from a dirty rug, this way it creates movement and contrast.
- **Snow Melt:** Create a bowl-shaped area in the snow (a couple feet wide and a foot deep) and lay the blanket over it. Then place small amounts of snow around edge of the bowl. As the sun's heat melts the snow, the resulting drinking water flows into the depression in the middle.
- **Sunshade:** To stay cool, hold the shiny side away from you for protection from the sun
- **Tent Cooling:** Keep your tent cooler in warm sunshine by draping Mylar over it to reflect the sun's heat and light
- **Tent Door:** Drape over doorway to allow passage while maintaining the temperature inside the tent
- **Warm Sack:** After wrapping in warm layers of clothing or sleeping bag, wrap yourself in the blanket like a burrito, with the shiny side facing in. Keeping the emergency blanket on the outside will block wind and trap body heat.
- **Water Collection from Dew:** Drape over vegetation and create valleys to collect dew overnight
- **Water Collection from Rain:** Dig a hole or build a frame and line it with the Mylar blanket to collect or hold rainwater. Similarly, tie the corners up to trees or bushes and place a weight at the center to create a large bowl that will collect rain water in the middle.

For similar uses, see the next Tools: Trash Bags section in this chapter.

Tools: Trash Bags

In addition to the previous **Tools: Mylar Blanket** section in this chapter, consider these utilizations for plastic trash bags when camping—whether made of black, white, orange, or clear plastic.

Capabilities & Principles

- Containers
- Watertight
- Airtight
- Cut into sheets, like Mylar blankets or tarps
- Cut into smaller pieces
- Blocks moisture
- Holds water

Remember that plastic does deteriorate and wear out over time—especially when exposed to sunlight, extreme temperatures, and repeated abrasions.

I recommend 55-gallon drum liners that are at least 1 mil thick.

Applications

- **Backpack Cover:** To supplement your personal rain gear
- **Bear Bag:** Tie food up out of reach from bears, and downwind from your campsite to avoid a bear encounter. This also keeps smaller critters out of your food overnight.
- **Bedding:** Fill with leaves or duff like a mattress
- **Blanket:** Like the Mylar Blankets in the previous section
- **Cordage:** Cut into strips and braid for lightweight rope
- **Dry Sack:** An extra layer of protection to keep electronics and clothing dry if you get caught in a rain storm or capsize your canoe. Zip-Tight Plastic Bags are better yet.
- **Dump Sack:** Keep handle to collect things on the move
- **Duvet:** Fill with leaves or duff and use like thick blanket
- **Emergency Backpack:** Enhance with frame of branches
- **Emergency Life Jacket:** Fill with air and cinch in middle for a quick support in a lake or river—for you, pets, gear, etc.

- **Emergency Poncho:** In rain or snow, protect yourself, your head, your backpack, your gear, your dog, or whatever!
- **Emergency Sleeping Bag or Bivy Shelter:** Be prepared with heavy duty, 95-gallon trash bags that you can crawl into during a rain storm like a Bivy bag.
- **Emergency Winter Coat:** Keep warmer—use by itself, between layers, or stuffed with insulation like leaves or duff
- **Firewood:** Keep dry from rain or snow
- **First Aid Cover:** Keep wounds clean and dry
- **First Aid Sling:** Fold into a triangle for an arm sling
- **Fish Catch:** Poke bag with as many holes as possible and use as net or trap to catch small fish
- **Floatation Device:** Fill two bags with air and tie together in an hourglass shape
- **Food Harvest Storage and Transport:** Keep fish, meat, plants, relatively clean until time to eat
- **Foot Wrap:** Keep feet dry by wrapping trash bags around feet, inside of shoes or boots
- **Gloves:** Keep hands clean for quick, messy jobs
- **Glue:** Heat with flame to shrink wrap or melt into liquid
- **Ground Cover:** Like a tarp, keep dampness off. Expand area by combining with duct tape.
- **Hat:** Keep of rain with a makeshift trash bag hat
- **Heat Water:** Keep black bag with water in direct sunlight
- **Ice Pack:** Fill with snow or ice to reduce swelling
- **Insulation Layer:** Keep warmer and dryer
- **Laundry Hamper:** Keep dirty clothes together
- **Patch with Duct Tape:** Repair most anything that needs to be nearly waterproof or airtight
- **Pillow:** Inflate and tie off for better sleep
- **Plates:** Place on flat rock for a relatively clean dinner plate
- **Poop Waste:** When you need temporary storage for proper disposal of personal or pet excrement.
- **Prep Mat:** Lay out flat for a relatively clean surface to prepare food or work on delicate projects
- **Seat Cover:** Lay on wet seating areas to keep pants dry

- **Shelter Material:** A moisture barrier to keep off rain and snow above, dampness below, or wind from sides
- **Shoe Bag:** Keep shoes wet or dry in backpack or luggage
- **Shower:** A black trash bag will warm water in sunlight; puncture several holes to stream like a showerhead
- **Signal Flag:** Attach a white bag to a pole for signaling
- **Sleeping Bag Liner:** Extra warmth and keep out wind
- **Snow Pants:** Tape around legs to keep dry in deep snow
- **Solar Water Still:** Make safe drinking water by evaporation
- **Spare Clothing:** Keep dry in a reusable trash bag
- **Splint:** Roll into tight tubes and tie around wounded limb
- **Stretcher:** Roll several bags like blanket between two poles
- **Sun Shade:** Attach to tree branches
- **Tablecloth:** Make a clean dinner table
- **Tarp:** See Tools: Tarps section in this chapter
- **Toilet Liner:** Sprinkle with dirt between uses & dispose of properly when finished
- **Trail Markers:** Cut into small strips and tie to tree branches
- **Transpiration Bag:** Wrap clear bag around tree branch or other plants to collect drinking water
- **Trash:** Of course you can use these to haul out your trash!
- **Tube Tent:** Support with rope/string between trees
- **Wash Clothes:** Add clothes, soap, and water; shake, squeeze, drain. Repeat with clean water to rinse.
- **Water Collection:** Catch rain or melt snow for drinking
- **Water Transport:** Use as a liner for larger volumes
- **Waterproof Gear:** Keep electronics safe from rain
- **Wet Clothing:** Keep the wet clothes wet and the dry clothes dry by keeping extra bags in your backpack.

*For similar uses, see the previous **Tools: Mylar Blanket** section in this chapter.*

Tools: Tarps

In addition to previous **Tools: Mylar Blanket** section and **Tools: Trash Bags** section in this chapter, consider these tarpaulin utilizations when camping.

Compare tarp sizes, weights, and prices

Capabilities & Principles

- Waterproof
- Windproof
- Durable
- Flexible
- Relatively clean
- Relatively light weight
- Block rain from above and moisture from below
- Shelter construction material

Materials

If you don't have an actual tarp, consider these alternatives.

- Tablecloth
- Shower Curtain
- Trash Bag
- Mylar Blanket
- Drop Cloth
- Insulation Sheeting
- Grill Cover
- Horse Blanket

Applications

- **Backpack:** Wrap with cording around makeshift frame
- **Bags:** Cut and sew into all shapes and sizes of bags
- **Bath:** Fill frame or dug-out hole for refreshing or steamy bath
- **Bathroom Privacy:** Make quick walls or roof for latrine
- **Bear Bag:** Wrap up and hang high (air tight would be better)
- **Bivy Sack:** Wrap up for a quick shelter on the ground

- **Boat Cover:** Keep gear dry while paddling canoe, kayak, etc.
- **Brush/Leaves Dragging:** To clear campsite or collect kindling
- **Campfire Protection:** Mount high & sloped to keep the rain off
- **Car/Trunk Liner:** Protect your car from wet & mud on gear
- **Field Dressing:** A clean surface for dressing harvested game
- **Flag:** Mount on large pole for signaling
- **Games:** Make targets for tossing gear like bean bags
- **Gifts:** For campers, hikers, & backpackers (or wrapping paper)
- **Ground Sheet:** A quick, dry spot for picnics, gear setup, etc.
- **Hammock:** Hang with rope; more comfortable than expected
- **Insulation:** If sleeping cold, add a layer of tarp around you
- **Kitchen Shelter:** Use instead of a tent when cooking in rain
- **Meat Wrap:** A wrapping to transport harvested game meat
- **Mud Cover:** Lay over muddy areas for cleaner tents & shoes
- **Patch:** Cover or glue patch for quick repair of a leaky roof
- **Pet Shelter:** They might not need a full tent, but dryer is better
- **Play Area:** for young children with toys
- **Poncho:** Wrap around yourself to keep you & pack dry
- **Quick Shelter:** Short-term rain/snow/sun protection for lunch
- **Rain Barrier:** An extra layer of protection for windy rain
- **Rain Cover:** Keep your equipment, gear, and firewood dry
- **Rain Water:** Collect for drinking water to refill your bottles
- **Rainfly:** Keep the rain off your hammock, tent, or eating area
- **Sail:** Give your boat an extra push from the wind
- **Shelter:** Create your own tent with a rainproof roof
- **Shower Stall:** Create walls for privacy
- **Sign:** Paint your name and hang like a billboard
- **Solar Still:** Make clean drinking water with evaporation or steam
- **Stretcher:** Wrap between two poles to carry someone
- **Sunshade:** Keep the sun off while cooking or resting
- **Tent Bottom:** Protect tent floor
- **Wind block:** Help with starting fire or escaping a cold wind

Tools: Cording

Cording, rope, string, floss, and similar tools can be essential for bush craft projects that add utility, safety, and comfort to any campsite. Consider these applications to help you decide if you need to carry some on your next outing.

*See the **Skills: Knot Tying** section in Chapter 6 for related information.*
Learn more about basic knot tying and practice regularly.

Paracord Applications

The most commonly used cording is **paracord**, which is short for parachute cord. This nylon rope is popular because of its strength (up to 550 pounds), small size, light weight, resistance to mold and mildew, and its ability to be separated into 14 smaller strands if needed.

Compare paracord colors, lengths, and prices: Tactical Paracord Options

- **Barrier:** Rope off an area to keep people away from danger
- **Barter:** Trade with others for essential supplies
- **Bear Bag:** Hang food from tree to keep way from wild animals
- **Belt:** Replace or support pants
- **Boot Traction:** Wrap around for better grip on wet surfaces
- **Bow Drill:** Start a fire using wooden drill
- **Bow String:** Emergency replacement
- **Bracelet:** Colorful style that can be untied for functionality
- **Bushcraft:** Dozens of fun and useful projects can be built for cooking, relaxing, crossing streams, hunting, weapons, etc.
- **Carry Strap:** Hold on to gear better
- **Chair:** Hang four corners of a towel from a tree
- **Clothes Line:** Use to hang wet clothes to dry
- **Color-Coded Wrapping** for labeling gear
- **Compression:** Make loose sacks tight and smaller
- **Dental Floss:** Finally get that popcorn out of your teeth
- **Dog Collar:** Stylish and versatile
- **Dog Leash:** Keep Fido under control

- **Drawstring Replacement:** Fix broken string in sweatpants, sweatshirts, or in drawstring bags
- **Fan Belt:** Wrap cordage tightly around the fan pulleys several times, and tie lots of knots around these loops of cordage, to make a single thick, knotty cord, which will help to reduce slippage while in use
- **Firewood Gathering:** Tie two 3′ lengths between two branches
- **Firewood Transport:** Wrap around branches to keep together
- **First Aid:** Tie splints around a broken limb, immobilize an arm, or use as a tourniquet
- **Fish Stringer:** Keep fish fresh by securing through the gills
- **Fishing:** Use the 14 inner strands for both the fishing line and to fashion a fly or lure
- **Fire Starter:** Not ideal, but better than nothing for tinder
- **Flashlight Hanger:** Free up your hands and light a larger area
- **Gaiters:** Tie pants tightly around boots to avoid ticks, snow, etc.
- **Gear Lanyard:** Tie expensive gear to yourself to avoid dropping, like eye glasses, camera, compass, binoculars, etc.
- **Glue:** Melt nylon with lighter and apply as glue
- **Grip:** Improve tool and weapon grip by wrapping around handle
- **Gun Cleaning:** Works as pull-through line for cleaning barrel
- **Gun Shooting Rest:** Tie paracord between two supports (like trees branches) to rest the rifle's fore-end and improve accuracy
- **Gun Sling:** Improvise to carry a shotgun or rifle
- **Hair Tie** or headband
- **Hammock Straps:** Repair or extend for greater distance
- **Hammocks:** Woven by itself, with other materials, or to tie off a blanket to be used as a hammock
- **Handcuffs:** Restrain bad guys
- **Handles:** Wrap hammer/hatchet to absorb shock on cold hands
- **Horse Halter and Bridle:** Replace, repair, lengthen
- **Hose Cleaning:** Tie knot & pull through pack hydration system
- **Hunting – Field Dressing:** Tie the animal's legs to tree branch for easier cleaning, dressing, skinning, butchering, etc.
- **Hunting – Game Transport:** Tie the animal's front and back legs together on each side to form handles, for easier carrying

- **Hunting Blind:** Use paracord to tie back weeds, brush, or tree limbs to create sniping or hunting loopholes
- **Jerky:** string up strips of game meat to dry over smoky fire
- **Keychain:** Stylish and versatile
- **Knife Handle:** Wrapped around solid steel knife
- **Ladder:** Tying branches together for the steps
- **Lantern Wick:** Emergency replacement
- **Lanyards:** Carry gear around your neck (with breakaway clasp)
- **Lashing:** Secure wooden structures and Bushcraft projects
- **Lasso:** Restrain animals and get under control
- **Leg Ties:** Wrap around leg to stabilize sheaths and holsters

TIP: To avoid frayed ends, use a lighter to melt and seal between fingers

- **Measuring:** Knotted measuring line, range finder, or plumb line
- **Pack:** Tie together branches to create a backpack
- **Packing:** Tie up rolled items like tarps and tents
- **Pull Cord:** Repair on snowmobile, chainsaw, boat, mower, etc.
- **Pulley System:** Use to lift heavy objects
- **Raft:** Lash logs together for a floating platform
- **Rappel:** Emergency rope to descend down a cliff or tree
- **Repairs:** Tie or wrap gear together
- **Rescue:** Toss to someone in water, mud, or pit to pull them out
- **Rock Sling:** Small game hunting or in search for Goliath
- **Rope:** Braid cord together for added strength or texture
- **Safety Line:** Use as a guideline for moving through dark caves, blizzard conditions, or other low visibility scenarios
- **Sailing:** Guy lines, mooring, towing, anchoring
- **Seal:** Melt nylon to seal holes in gear
- **Seat:** Lash a horizontal log between two trees
- **Sewing:** Use inner strands to repair backpack, tent, clothing, etc.
- **Shelter:** Lash poles together for shelter structure
- **Shelter:** Tie up a poncho or Mylar blanket for shelter
- **Shoelaces:** Replace or lengthen shoe or boot laces
- **Snares:** Emergency food harvesting
- **Snow Shoes:** Tie branches in place and to your feet
- **Spear:** Lash a knife to a long stick

- **Strapping:** Add more gear to the outside of your backpack
- **Strapping:** Repair or lengthen backpack straps & belt, bra, etc.
- **Suspenders:** Hold up your pants when a belt won't do
- **Tent Guy Lines:** Repair, replace, or lengthen
- **Tie Down:** Keep things in place during a wind storm
- **Tie Downs:** Secure large loads on pickup truck or in car trunk
- **Tire Chains:** Emergency traction for your vehicle
- **Tool Belt:** Secure gear to your waist
- **Tow Lines:** For vehicles, four wheelers, boats, etc.
- **Trap:** Devise various snares to catch small game
- **Trip Wire:** Protect an area with bells or noisy cans
- **Water Collection:** Run a line of cord from a damp surface into a water bottle to collect the water one drip at a time
- **Zip Line:** Use as a line for a dog run, or tied between two trees to make a horse hitching line
- **Zipper Pull:** Replace broken zipper tab
- **Gift:** A 50-foot bolt or 1000-foot roll makes a great gift for campers, outdoorsmen, hunters, and more.

Visit buckonbeach "A Long-Term Survival Guide - 101 Uses for Paracord" site for detailed illustrations of more uses of paracord.

Shock Cord

Also known as bungee cord or shock cord, this elastic rope can be found in various sizes, strengths, and colors. Some come with hooks on the ends, while others come in spools for you to customize. It is great for securing items quickly without knots. While not usually essential, its ability to give and stretch under tension make it ideal for specific applications, like the following.

- Around cuffs of jacket, coat, poncho, etc.
- Around waist of jacket, sweatshirt, raincoat, etc.
- Attach bulky items outside of backpack, like jacket or rain gear
- Hammock under quilt
- Hammock utility straps
- Restraining cargo during transport
- Securing tarps or rain fly in windy conditions

Rope

Heavier than most other cording, consider the following types of rope to meet your needs.

- **Binder/Baling twine:** cheap, strong, lashing
- **Braided:** strong and stretchy
- **Climbing:** durable and tear resistant
- **Cotton:** nice handling and resistant to sunlight, but poor when it comes to shock load or resisting mildew and rot (store dry)
- **Manila:** strong, easy-to-handle, can be spliced; Compared to others, works great when left in sunlight (store dry)
- **Nylon:** strong, elastic (usually 20%), tends to slip; Compared to others, works best for durability, handling, shock load, and resisting abrasion, gas, mildew, oil, and rot (store wet or dry)
- **Polyester:** more expensive, nice handling for knot practice; Compared to others, works best for durability and handling, and resisting abrasion, acid, rot, gas, mildew, oil, and sunlight (store wet or dry)
- **Polyethylene:** cheap, floats
- **Polypropylene:** cheap, floats, water resistant, minimal stretch; Compared to others, works poorly when left in sunlight and works best for being lightweight and resisting acid, rot, gas, mildew, and oil (store wet or dry)
- **Sisal:** stiff, natural fiber, kinks, breaks down when wet; Compared to others, works great when left in sunlight (store dry)

Inspect rope frequently to find any frays that may diminish the rope's strength or reliability.

Remember these important rope factors.

- **Strength When Knotted:** Any knot in rope reduces its strength by up to 20%. An overhand knot, which cuts into itself, reduces rope strength by 50%.
- **Strength When Exposed:** Polypropylene ropes lose strength with extended sunlight exposure.
- **Working Load:** Usually is 20% of a rope's breaking strength

- **Fraying:** To minimize fraying when cutting a rope, wrap about two inches of the rope tightly with tape and then cut in the middle of the tape.
- **Fraying:** To minimize fraying of a poly, nylon, or synthetic rope, use a small flame to melt the frayed ends into a single ball.

Zip Ties

Also called cable ties and duct straps, zip ties have so many uses when camping, hiking, or backpacking, that they are almost as essential as duct tape. You can find them in various lengths, colors, and strengths. Consider these uses for zip ties when you are away from home.

- **Bag Closure:** Weave around bag opening and pull tight
- **Boot Laces:** For repairs, replacement, or reinforcement
- **Boot Traction:** Wrap around for better grip on wet surfaces
- **Bushcraft:** Dozens of fun and useful projects can be built for cooking, relaxing, crossing streams, hunting, weapons, etc.
- **Carry Strap:** Hold on to gear better
- **Clothing:** Keep everything packed tightly, or grouped by day
- **Color Coding:** Use to organize things by color of zip tie (red=fire, blue=water, green=food, etc.)
- **First Aid:** Use to wrap splint, hold sling, secure bandage
- **Fish Stringer:** Keep fish fresh by securing through the gills
- **Flashlight Hanger:** Free up your hands and light a larger area
- **Gaiters:** Wrap around ankle cuffs to keep out snow, ticks, etc.
- **Hair Tie** to pull hair back
- **Handcuffs:** Secure hands or feet to prevent escape
- **Hooks:** Use to attach anything to your backpack, tent, etc.
- **Ice Cleats:** Wrap around boots for extra traction
- **Key Chain:** Hold keys and gadgets together
- **Key Spare:** Tie spare key into bag, backpack, under car, etc.
- **Lashing:** Hold brush craft projects together
- **Lock:** Secure things from animals and leave tampering evidence
- **Pack:** Tie together branches to create a backpack
- **Packing:** Tie up rolled items like tarps and tents

- **Repairs:** Re-attach straps, ropes, tears, tents, backpacks, clothing
- **Secrets:** Color code messages like stop, need water, etc.
- **Shelter:** Lash multiple tarps together for a rainproof roof
- **Shelter:** Lash pieces of an improvised shelter together
- **Shelter:** Lash saplings together for a teepee frame
- **Shelter:** Tie up a poncho or Mylar blanket for shelter
- **Shoelaces:** Replace or lengthen shoe or boot laces
- **Snare:** Improvise traps to capture wild animals
- **Snow Shoes:** Tie branches in place and to your feet
- **Spear:** Lash a knife to a long stick
- **Strapping:** Add more gear to the outside of your backpack
- **Trail Marker:** Hang on tree limbs to mark your trail
- **Wrench:** Wrap around a bolt to tighten or loosen
- **Zipper Pulls:** Extend or replace zipper pulls for better grip

Some zip ties or much stronger than others!
Also, exposure to sun or heat reduces strength.

Tools: Duct Tape

Strong, sticky, waterproof, and air-tight—duct tape (or duck tape) can be used for so many things—giving it the name, "The Ultimate Survival Tool." You've probably heard lots of stories about the many uses of duct tape (DT). Here's a list of ideas for quick reference.

Capabilities & Principles

- Adhesive
- Binding
- Patching
- Cording
- Repairing
- Flexible
- Clothing Repair
- First Aid

Duct tape contains three layers: 1) plastic, 2) fabric mesh, 3) adhesive.

Applications

- Backpack Belt Padding with T-shirt
- Backpack Repair
- Bandage Making with tissue paper
- Bandage Waterproofing
- Belt Replacement
- Bivy Building with trash bags
- Blabbermouth Muting
- Blister Care & Protection
- Boat Repair
- Boot Insole Insulation
- Boot Laces
- Boot Repair
- Bushcraft
- Cactus Needle Extraction
- Clothesline
- Clothing Repair

- Container Sealing and Waterproofing
- Cording
- Deputy: Restrain/handcuff/muzzle a captured criminal
- Dishware: Create a water-tight cup, bowl, or plate
- Draft Blocking
- Drinking Cup Crafting
- Fire Starter
- Fishing Pole Repair with splint
- Fly Paper to catch bugs
- Food Package Resealing
- Gaiters
- Glasses Repair
- Glove Repair or Reinforcement
- Guy Line Building or Repair
- Hammock Building
- Handcuffs
- Handle Grip
- Hang Gear and Lights
- Hat Crafting
- Hose Repair
- Hunting: Attach knife (spear), gig (frogs, fish), to long pole
- Inflatables: Repair inner tube, tire, boat, sleeping pad
- Injury: Buddy tape broken fingers or toes together
- Mouse Trap
- Pant Hemming
- Patch: Fix leaky boat, kayak, tubing, or bladder
- Pillow: Secure zip-tight plastic bags with clothing
- Rain Gear Repair
- Rain Shelter: Use large garbage bags and duct tape
- Rappelling Harness
- Rope and Cording
- Rope Fray Repair
- Sandals and Flip Flop Crafting
- Seam and Edge Binding for tarps and groundsheets
- Shelter Building
- Shoe Waterproofing

- Shoelace Repair
- Sleeping Bag Repair
- Sling for Injured Arm
- Snowshoe Building
- Spear Making
- Splinter Removal
- Sprained Ankle Splint
- Sunglasses: Like a blindfold with narrow slits to cut sun glare
- Tablecloth Attachment
- Tent Closure with broken zipper
- Tent Fabric Repair
- Tent Pole Repair with splint
- Tie Downs
- Trail Markers
- Water Bottle Repair
- Water Bucket: Retrieve water and keep near campfire
- Waterproofing: Use with plastic bags to seal anything
- Webbing: Use for rifle sling or hammock straps
- Windbreak with trash bags
- Wound Stitching and Covering
- Zipper Pull Replacement
- Zipper Repair

Attach extra duct tape around gear instead of lugging a big roll of it. Consider a flashlight, tent pole, backpack frame, plastic bags, water bottle, or gift card.

Tools: Sunshade Visor

Going by many names—Car Visor, Sun Visor, Automobile Reflector Protector, or Foldable Windshield Sun Shade, these rectangular Sunshade Visors are designed to block sunlight from your windshield and keep your vehicle cooler. They are also great to have when you're camping and I always take one with me!

Save Money: You can easily spend $10 to $20 for one of these, but I get mine from the Dollar-type Store.

Capabilities & Principles

- Flat and sturdy
- Relatively clean
- Waterproof
- Windproof
- Insulated
- Padded
- Floats
- Reflects light and heat
- Flexible—starts stiff and softens with use

Sunshades usually have four layers: 1) a shiny side, 2) bubble wrap for insulation, 3) cardboard for stiffness and strength, and 4) a strong back side.

Applications

- **Backpack Frame:** Line inside of backpack for added stiffness
- **Colder Food:** Wrap around food bags in your backpack
- **Dry Clothes:** Place clothes on reflective visor in sunlight
- **Electronics:** Project from water, heat, light, shock, vibration
- **Emergency Backpack:** Fold and secure with duct tape straps
- **First Aid:** Use to immobilize injured arms and legs
- **Floatation Device:** Fold under shirt for extra buoyancy
- **Food Tray:** Use like a serving tray to pass food or eat in your lap
- **Hammock Pad:** Keep warm and hold diagonal shape
- **Heat Reflector:** Place campfire in front of you and reflector behind you—so you feel radiated heat all around you
- **Heat Reflector:** Place on far side of campfire for more heat

- **Insulation:** Use inside sleeping bag for added thermal barrier
- **Level Table:** Place drinks, soups, pots where they won't tip over
- **Mat:** Stand on when changing clothes or boots to keep feet dry
- **Packing:** Use as padding in backpack to stop clinking noise
- **Pillow:** Wrap around clothing and rest your head on it
- **Rain Collection:** Direct rainwater into drinking bottle
- **Rain Hat:** Hold over your head for quick rain protection
- **Rain Protection:** Place over gear, firewood, pet
- **Seat Padding:** Attach to canoe or kayak seats
- **Seat:** Sit on to keep warm, dry, and comfortable
- **Shelter Roof:** Keep rain off of emergency shelter or Bivy
- **Signaling:** Use shiny side to reflect sunlight
- **Sleep Pad:** Use under sleeping bag to keep warm & dry
- **Smoking:** Create a smoke tent to preserve meat
- **Snow Melt:** Place snow on reflective visor in sunlight
- **Solar Cooking:** Reflect sunlight to intensify heat in solar oven
- **Solar Still:** Collect steam and condense into drinking water
- **Sun Block:** Protect tent from hot sun
- **Sun Block:** Quick protection from hot sun
- **Tablecloth:** Lay out for a dining table or cooking prep area
- **Thermal Pad:** Use on sandy beach to protect from heat of sand
- **Welcome Mat:** Use in front of tent or hammock for wet boots
- **Wind Block:** Help get fire started or protect stove flames
- **Wind Collection:** Funnel air into a struggling campfire
- **Wind Redirection:** Focus wind to dry clothing or skin

Tools: Cargo Net

Capabilities

- Bush Craft Support: chair, cot, hammock
- Cargo Net
- Climbing Tool
- Collection Bag
- Dunk Bag: cleaning laundry or dishes in stream
- Emergency Coat or Blanket
- Emergency Raft or Float
- Emergency Shelter Material
- Fishing Net
- Ghillie Blanket
- Ghillie Hide
- Ghillie Suit
- Hammock: for you, supplies, or a bear stash
- Secure a Door, Window, or Funnel Passage
- Snare
- Stretcher
- Trap

Applications

- Carry harvested game back to camp
- Clean laundry, dishes, or food in a river or pond
- Collect bundle firewood
- Consider small metal "S" hooks for quick and easy attachments
- Hoist food & gear up out of reach of bear, varmint, children
- Preserve or cool food submersed under water
- Raise or lower gear into a tree or down a cliff
- Weave foliage into the net for camouflage
- Weave in plastic bags or newspaper for insulation

Tools: Cattails

Cattail plants (or bulrushes or reeds) are easily identified and found near most any water source—streams, lake shores, ponds, ditches, and swamps. It is not only edible, it can be used for insulation, basket weaving, bedding, cordage, and much more.

Food

Cattail stalks and roots are rich in vitamins A, B, and C; potassium and phosphorus.

- **Stems:** Best in early summer, cut the stems just a few inches above the soil; peel and eat raw (or boil like potatoes)
- **Roots:** Pull lower stalks out of the ground to reveal the roots; peel and eat raw, roast, or boil like potatoes (spit out the chewy fibers)

Peel roots while they are still wet; it becomes difficult when they are dry.

- **Heads:** Roast the flower heads like an ear of corn
- **Pollen:** Best in summer or early fall, collect pollen from the heads and use like flour to make breads, pancakes, or to thicken sauces.
- **Starch:** Pull up the roots, clean, mash, and soak to release starch, which settles to the bottom of the liquid; use for bread with pollen or make soup.

One of the best parts is the new shoots off the main root. They start out looking like an alligator's tooth, then a pointed hook—three or four inches long.

- **Scalloped Cattails:** Starting with two cups chopped cattail tops—put into a bowl with a half cup of melted butter, two beaten eggs, a pinch of sugar, a pinch of nutmeg, and a pinch of black pepper. Blend and slowly add a cup of hot milk to the mixture. Pour into a greased casserole dish and top with grated Swiss cheese. Bake 275 degrees for half an hour.
- **Cattail Pollen Pancakes:** Mix a half cup cattail pollen, a half cup flour, one cup of milk, one egg, two tablespoons baking powder, one teaspoon salt, three tablespoon bacon drippings. Pour into a hot skillet to make small pancakes.

Shelter

- **Shingles:** Cut the green leaves and weave together into squares to cover your shelter roof
- **Sleeping Mat:** Weave the green leaves into two long mats; fill space between them with insulating material like evergreen branches or leaves, and then bind the edges for an insulating floor mat

Medicinal

- **Ointment:** Split open a cattail root, crush the exposed area, and apply to skin to soothe scrapes, burns, and insect bites.
- **Antiseptic Salve:** To treat wounds, stings, or toothaches, use the ashes of burnt cattails or the sticky, honey-like substance that seeps from the cattail stem—which is also a coagulant and mild numbing agent.
- **Bleeding:** Use the hemostatic & astringent pollen to control bleeding in an open cut or wound. Take internally for menstrual pain.
- **Diarrhea:** Drink tea of hot water and root flour, or eat the flower heads, to help treat dysentery and diarrhea.

Basket Weaving

- Weave the long green leaves into baskets, pouches, packs, and more for carrying food, berries, bait, and more.
- Start by weaving a large square, then fold into the desired shape before weaving around the sides to secure the shape. The container will become stronger and stiffer as the leaves dry and harden.

Cordage

- Strip, cut, or peel the long green leaves into narrow strips and allow them to dry somewhat before braiding.
- Use this cordage for lashing bush craft, securing shelter structures, fishing, mending, and more.

Fire

- **Starter:** Tear apart the dark cattail head to expose the dry fluff inside, which makes great tinder when starting a campfire.
- **Torch:** Roll the cattail head in pine resin to create a torch for light.
- **Drill:** Use a dried stalk shaft as a hand drill for friction fire starting.

Insulation or Padding

Tear apart the dark cattail head to expose the dry fluff inside, which can be used for insulation or padding in boots, shoes, hats, mittens, sleeping bags, mattresses, or pillows.

Tools: Plastic Bottles

Plastic bottles of all shapes and sizes are readily available almost anywhere—whether you take them with you or you just find them along the way. If you find yourself needing extra resource utilization, consider these unexpected uses from everyday bottles.

Applications

- **Cordage:** Cut a long, spiraling piece of plastic ¼-inch wide—use for things like fishing line, lashing cord, snare trapping, shoe lace, or a tent line. Note that the plastic in larger 2-liter bottles is much thicker than smaller bottles, so it is not as flexible.
- **Cup or Bowl:** Cut around middle to create a drinking cup or bowl from bottom.
- **Faucet:** Hang upside down and slowly unscrew the cap to the desired flow rate, like just a trickle for washing hands.
- **Feet:** Cut oval hole in the side, near the bottom of a 2-liter bottle, just big enough for your foot (with or without shoe) and stuff the space between your foot and the bottle with any sort of insulation (dry grass, cattail fuzz, dry moss, clothing, foam, etc.)—keep your feet dry when walking through water or mud, or warm when in snow or while sleeping.
- **Fire:** A clear plastic bottle with water can be used to focus sunlight onto tinder and start a fire. You will also need some patience and practice.
- **Float Marker:** Recap bottle and tie string around neck to find something underwater, like a case of cold drinks or a jug of milk.
- **Floatation Device:** Tie enough bottles together and you can get most anything to float, which can help with river crossing.
- **Food Storage:** Reuse an empty water bottle to pack ice, soup, sauce, oil, milk, eggs, or other drinks in your backpack.
- **Foot Care:** Whether using with hot or cold water, lay 2-liter bottle on its side and cut a hole large enough for your foot to be submerged for cleaning, warming, or cooling your feet.

- **Foot Fungi:** Cure athlete's foot and other foot fungus by soaking your feet in urine collected in a plastic bottle—the ammonia in the urine kills the fungus.
- **Funnel:** Cut around middle to create a funnel from the top neck. Use when mechanically filtering water for drinking by using cloth, paper, charcoal, sand, etc. Use to pour fuel into a camp stove. Use to pour water between canteens or water bottles. Use to get rainwater from tent or tarp into water bottle.
- **Rain Collection:** If you have nothing else to funnel the rain into the bottle, cut in half lengthwise for maximum surface area.
- **Resealable Bags:** Cut off top (neck and cap) and screw around the opening of a small plastic bag to make it resealable—use for snacks, cereal, liquids, powders, rice, sugar, and more.
- **Sandals:** Make emergency footwear with bottles & cording.
- **Scoop:** Cut off top neck and use the bottom to shovel sand, dirt, water, mud, etc.
- **Spoon:** Cut from bottom of bottle, where the folds of plastic are already formed like spoons.
- **Waterproof Canister:** Cut two bottle necks and glue them together so that the screw caps are at either end—use for matches, fire starter, batteries, and more.
- **Wind Turbine Blades:** You can either cut bottles around the middle like funnels, or cut lengthwise like fan blades.
- **Wisk Broom:** Cut off bottom and shred the middle portion into long strips, creating a small broom held by the neck—use this to clean out your tent, clear an area for your campfire, and more.
- **Warm Sleeping Bag:** Pour warm water into bottles, cap tightly, and place in sleeping bag to keep warm—especially around feet.

Fishing

- **Fish Bobber:** Tie one end of fishing line to bottle and bait a hook on the other end—be sure you can retrieve once a fish is hooked.
- **Fish Line:** Cut a long, spiraling piece of plastic about ¼-inch wide or less.

- **Fish Lure:** Cut plastic into fizzy strips, somewhat like a spider, and secure to hook using cording made from plastic water bottle.
- **Fish Reel:** Tie end of fishing line to neck of bottle, then wrap several yards of fishing line around middle of the bottle, and use like a fish pole to cast the line off the end of the bottle—wrapping around the bottle keeps the line from knotting up and retrieving is much faster.
- **Fish Trap:** Cut off top neck and invert top into middle, add bait inside, secure with wire, string, or fishing line. Works best for minnows and crayfish.

Purifying Water

If a plastic bottle is the only thing you have to hold water, there are still options for using it and heat to purify water. Your goal is to get the water above 180 degrees for several minutes. A word of caution, however, in that a slight misjudgment in heat or placement may ruin an otherwise good water container.

- **Pasteurize:** Completely fill the bottle with water, cap it tightly, and place the full bottle in some hot coals. The water inside and lack of air should prevent the water from boiling and the plastic from melting.
- **Pasteurize:** Suspend a plastic water bottle just above flames or coals, and bring the water almost to a boil, so that the water inside keeps the plastic from melting.
- **Solar Disinfection:** Leave the water bottle in bright sunshine for several hours to help kill any bacteria or parasites from the sun's heat, light radiation, and ultralight rays.
- **Hourglass Bottle Still:** Fill a water bottle one-third full of unpurified water. Tape another bottle to this bottle at the mouth, so that together they look like an hourglass. Please these bottles in direct sunlight at a slight angle so that evaporated water from the lower side can cool and collect in the upper side.
- **Bottle Trough Still:** Cut bottom off of a clean, plastic bottle—the larger the better. Roll up the bottom edge so that it curls inward, creating a trough around the inside, about an inch deep. If

needed, use heat from a flame to help mold the plastic. Place this still, with cap in place, over something wet and in direct sunlight. If needed, use string to suspend this still over unclean water that is being heated. As evaporation (or steam) rises and condenses on the sides of the bottle, it will collect in the trough. To drink, twist off the cap and drink like any water bottle. Repeat as needed.

Tools: Cooking Supplies

Cooking Oil

Consider these ideas for using and utilizing this all-purpose tool, whether vegetable oil, olive oil, peanut oil, or any other cooking oil.

- **Add to Dried Foods** – improves taste and texture
- **Blisters** – apply at night to heal faster
- **Breads Topping** – a tasty dip, especially with dried seasonings
- **Butter Alternative** – adds flavor and calories
- **Clean Dishes** – just add a few drops and scrub instead of soap
- **Cookware Sticking** – to avoid food sticking
- **Insect Repellent** – avoid being bitten by bugs
- **Laxative** – an extra teaspoon may loosen stools
- **Shave** – use like shaving cream to lubricate shaving blade
- **Skin Cleanser** – to remove dirt and grime, then rinse with water
- **Skin Lubricant** – prevent chafing wherever it is being rubbed
- **Skin Moisturizer** – including chapped lips
- **Snoring** – keeps throat moist and lubricated to reduce snoring
- **Soothe Sunburn** – avoid skin peeling
- **Tool Lubricant** – keep folding knife, can opener working well
- **Warm Up** – drink a teaspoon to warm and soothe a cold body
- **Zipper Lubricant** – just a drop works wonders

Coffee Filters

These ultra-light weight and inexpensive paper coffee filters have many uses when you are camping.

- **Bandage:** Cover wound with filter and tape
- **Bugs:** Keep bugs out of supplies by filling a filter with cedar
- **Clean Glass:** Filters are lint-free for cleaning glasses
- **Cloth Diaper Liner:** For easier cleanup and washing
- **Coffee:** Well, of course, you can make coffee with coffee filters
- **Disposable Bowls:** For kid's snacks, like popcorn and chips
- **Dust Mask Pre-Filter:** Extend the life of your respirator filter
- **Hardware Organization:** Keep screws, bolts, nuts, etc. sorted

- **Ingredients:** Hold pre-measured cooking ingredients
- **Paper:** Draw a map, remember a number, leave a message
- **Parts Protection:** Hold small pieces safely while repairing gear
- **Plate/Bowl:** Hold snacks and sandwiches in dirty hands
- **Protect Food:** From flying bugs and bees
- **Spoon Rest:** Keep your utensils clean when cooking
- **Tea Filter:** Fill with all sorts of tea, flowers, or herbal infusions
- **Tinder:** Use to start fire, especially soaked in oil, grease, Vaseline
- **Toilet paper:** Alternative backup plan
- **Water Filter:** First stage for purifying drinking water—in funnel, covering mouth of bottle, over straw, or covering a commercial filter system to extend the life of the filters

Aluminum Foil

Sometimes called "tin foil," aluminum foil is a versatile tool to keep on hand. Several types are available, in various thicknesses and sizes.

Capabilities & Principles

- Waterproof
- Airproof
- Non-combustible (will not burn)
- Flexible
- Electrical Conductor
- Shiny, Reflective

Applications

- Ashes Cleanup: place under fire before starting
- Bake Food in a bed of hot coals
- Battery tightening: add wad of foil to improve connectivity
- Block Wind next to camp stove
- Bug Blocking Lid over drinks
- Char Cloth Crafting for next campfire
- Cooking Container & Wrapper
- Dishware Crafting: plate, cup, spoon
- Dry Wrap for matches, tinder, food, medicine, etc.
- Fishing Lure Crafting

- Fry Food over a campfire
- Funnel Crafting with extra flexibility
- Grill Cleaning
- Insulation to keep containers of food warm or cold
- Lost Lid Replacement
- Matches Wrapper
- Reflector behind lights, candles, campfire
- Rust Removal from grill, tools, or equipment
- Scrubber for pots and pans
- Tool Sharpening for knives, scissors, blades
- Trail Markers that are easy to see at night with flashlight

Tools: What's in Your Pockets?

Knowing how to utilize everyday items on hand—for unintended purposes, can be essential when you have limited resources and unexpected needs. You might find these items may be in your coat pocket, purse, fanny pack, backpack, vehicle, etc.

Hand Sanitizer

Hand Sanitizer lotion (also called Alcohol Wipes, Antibacterial Wipes, Hand Sanitizer Wipes, and more) is available in containers of many shapes and sizes. The most common forms are gels and wipes.

- **Clean Hands:** Use before eating, after using toilet, etc.
- **Clean Dishes:** Wash cookware, silverware, serving dishes, etc.
- **Clean Eyeglasses:** Including goggles, sunglasses, binoculars, etc.
- **Remove Grease:** Mix with salt and water to clean hands
- **Stain Remover:** Rub into stain to remove it, then wash in water
- **First Aid:** Clean minor cuts and abrasions to disinfect
- **Bug Bites:** Apply to mosquito bites to reduce pain & itching
- **Glue Remover:** Apply a tiny amount to loosen dried glue
- **Fire Starter:** Lights quickly and burns hot, especially the wipes

For fire starting, look for a higher alcogel or alcohol percentage (91% vs. 35%).

Super Glue

Cyanoacrylate, or Super Glue, is amazingly strong for a number of applications in the woods. I recommend the single-use packs.

Nail polish remover (acetone) will remove superglue from fingers.

- **First Aid:** Seal skin for cuts or wounds—instead of bandages. Pinch skin together and apply minimal glue on top; do not fill the gap in between the skin.
- **Repairs:** Fix just about anything that might break or separate: tent, backpack, plastic buckles, electronics, cookware, boots...

Unopened, the shelf life of superglue is at least one year.

Lip Balm (ChapStick)

Originally intended as a skin moisturizer that helps protect chapped, sunburned, or wind-burned lips, lip balm ingredients like aloe, vitamin E, beeswax, and other medicinal components give it other benefits and potential utilizations that could apply to any form of this material—in a tube, jar, tin, tub, or pouch.

- **Face Warmer**: Apply in extreme cold to limit heat loss
- **Finger Splint**: Cut empty ChapStick tube in half lengthwise
- **Fire Starter**: Add to Cotton, lint, gauze, cloth, or dry vegetation like petroleum jelly to receive sparks and light a fire
- **First Aid**: Apply to wound to stop bleeding and keep clean
- **Knot-tying**: Apply before cinching to lock into place
- **Light**: Add string or Cotton for wick and use as a candle
- **Light Lantern**: Place lit "candle" in a tin can that has been cut open and spread apart to reflect light and hold the lit tube
- **Lubricant**: Apply to stubborn zippers, fishing rod joints, fire bow drill, rusty bolts, or foot blisters
- **Matchbox**: An used/empty ChapStick tube is water-resistant for matches, tinder, or other small items
- **Mini-Torch**: Apply to one end of a Cotton swab stick (like Q-Tips) for a torch that burns brightly for several minutes
- **Rust Proofing**: rub on knives, zippers, and other equipment
- **Shoelaces**: Apply to lace knot to keep footwear tied up tight
- **Skin**: Dry lips AND wind-blown ears, cheeks, noses, elbows, joints, hands, fingers, cuticles
- **Soothe Rashes & Bug Bites**: Less itch & promotes healing
- **Water Proofing**: Temporary patch to tent, fly, tarp, rain gear
- **Water Sealing**: Improve water resistance by applying to seals of flashlights, electronics, boxes, or canisters

Bandana

Going by many names, these have so many great improvised uses when you're outdoors: handkerchief, kerchief, neckerchief, bandana, babushka, do-rag, madras, shawl, or hankie.

Uses

- **Bear Bag** with string/rope to loft into a tree
- **Belt or Strap**
- **Bib** to keep shirt clean
- **Blindfold** to improve sleep
- **Camp Markers** for trails, landmarks, territories, warnings
- **Campfire Windscreen** to get the first started on a windy day
- **Carrying Pouch**
- **Cooling Wrap** by soaking in water and wearing around neck
- **Cording** by tearing into strips and braiding
- **Deter Wild Animals**: urinate on pieces & place around campsite
- **Dry Feet** after crossing a stream
- **Dust Mast**
- **Ear Muffs** for reducing noise or keeping warm
- **Eye Cover** for a daytime nap
- **Feminine Hygiene** or Pee Wipe
- **Flashlight Cover** to dim your light
- **Fly Swatter**
- **Foot Warmer** by wrapping hot rocks for sleeping bag
- **Glasses Cleaning**
- **Group Identifier** by tying on packs or arms of everyone
- **Halter Top** using two, folded into triangles, and tied off
- **Hand Wrap** to protect against blisters, cuts, or dirt
- **Handkerchief**
- **Hat**, keeping hair out of face, protection from sun, etc.
- **Head Wrap** for sweat, rain, hair
- **Key Chain** by tying corner to key
- **Knee Pad**
- **Lashing** to hold bush craft sticks together
- **Neck Protection** by tucking under cap or hat
- **Net** to capture or hold things, like collecting berries or minnows
- **Nose Blowing**
- **Occupied Signal** for Outhouse or Latrine Area
- **Pack** or Stuff Sack
- **Padding** for fragile items in pack

- **Pillow** by stuffing with socks or clothing
- **Pouch** for small items in pack
- **Scarf** for warmth, bugs, rain
- **Short Rope** or tie and twist for longer rope
- **Sitting Cloth** to keep pants clean & dry
- **Sneeze or Cough Muffler**
- **Sunshade**
- **Sweatband** on wrist, arm, or head
- **Sweaty Hand Drying**
- **Toothbrush**
- **Towel** to dry things off; tie outside of backpack to dry
- **Trail Marker**
- **Washcloth**
- **Water Filter**, Pre-Filter, or First-Stage Water Filter
- **Wind Direction Check** for placement of campfire, tent, etc.
- **Wind Mask** in cold weather

Cooking & Eating

- **Apron** to keep clothes clean
- **Bug Cover** to project your food, drink, etc.
- **Coffee Filter**
- **Dish Scrubber**
- **Jar Opening** for better grip of lid
- **Napkin**
- **Pasta Strainer**
- **Plate**
- **Pot Holder**
- **Salad Spinner** to remove moisture from washed greens
- **Sponge**
- **Strainer**
- **Tablecloth** or Placemat
- **Tea Filter** or Teabag

Emergency

- **Baby Diaper**
- **Char Cloth** for future fire building

- **Dew Collector** for drinking water
- **Dog Collar** or **Dog Leash** (tied together)
- **Fire Starter**, Kindling
- **Flagging** someone for help
- **Footwear Insole** for replacement or extra padding
- **Gloves** to keep hands warm
- **Ice Pack** with snow, icicles, ice cubes, etc.
- **Lamp Wick**
- **Pack Strap** Replacement
- **Patch** to mend clothing
- **Shoelaces** or bootlaces, after cutting or ripping into strips
- **Signal Flag** to get attention or help
- **Smoke Signaling**
- **Socks**
- **Swim Trunks** & Bikini
- **Toilet Paper** that can be washed and re-used
- **Trail Marker** for others to find you or to return the way you came
- **Water Filter** to remove sediment and dirt from drinking water

First Aid

- **Compress** (hot or cold)
- **Eye Patch**
- **Finger Splint/Wrap**
- **Foot Wrap**
- **Poultice**
- **Sling** for arm
- **Splint Tie**
- **Tourniquet**
- **Washcloth**
- **Wrap/Brace** (knee, ankle, elbow, wrist, etc.)

Hand Warmers

These are the chemically activated heating pads, sometimes including an adhesive, and least expensive when purchased in bulk in the spring or summer.

- **Battery Life**: Wrap around battery compartment of camera, phone, or other electronic devices to help it last longer
- **Boot Drying**: Place one in each boot overnight
- **Canister Stove**: Use as base for stove/fuel to work better
- **Drink Snow**: Use to melt snow into drinkable water
- **Hot Drink**: Wrap around mug to keep warmer longer
- **Hypothermia**: Use under armpits or groin to warm body
- **Reduce Moisture**: Place USED hand warmer in bag with electronic devices to pull moisture out of the equipment
- **Sleeping Bag**: Place in the foot of bag an hour before sleeping
- **Soothing**: Apply to sore muscles to relieve pain
- **Water Bottle**: Use to keep water from freezing in your pack

Tampons

- **Eye Glass** cleaning
- **Compression Bandage**: Stop bleeding and keep sterile
- **Ear Plugs**: Protection from firearms, snoring, wind, etc.
- **Fire Starter** material
- **Fuel Spill**: Absorb stove fuel or any other liquid
- **Nose Bleeds**: Stop bleeding and avoid spreading blood
- **Toothbrush**: Rub with finger
- **Water Filter**: Remove large debris

Dental Floss

- **Cording**: Build tools, furniture, weapons, shelters
- **Fire Starter** (waxed floss)
- **Fishing Line**: Wrap around plastic bottle to reel/cast
- **Hang Clothing** to dry in breeze or near campfire
- **Knife**: Use for semi-hard items like cheese, fruit, clay
- **Netting**: Mend mosquito or fish netting
- **Rope**: Braid as needed for added strength
- **Shoelace** or bootlace
- **Thread**: Heavy-duty for tent, backpack, socks, skin, etc.

Zip-tight Plastic Bags

Not all plastic zip-tight plastic bags are equal!

- **Thickness** is typically measured from 1 Mil (lightweight) to 8 Mil (heavy duty). "Freezer" bags tend to be thicker and more durable.
- **The Zipper** can be a single our double, with our without a slider.
- **Various Sizes** can be purchased online, especially in bulk. They can be very small to carry cooking ingredients, or very large to hold clothing.
- **Sucking Air Out** of zip-tight plastic bags with clothing or soft gear helps reduce space in your backpack.
- **Keywords** for searching (depending on your needs) may include words like "plastic, storage, bags, zip, zipper, Ziploc, reclosable, disposable, freezer"
- **Popular Brands** include Glad, Hefty, Ziploc, Elkay, and Plymor.

See samples of Ziploc plastic bags here.

Socks

Some tools you may not likely ever carry with you, but more than likely you WILL have socks on during your next great adventure.

Improvised Uses

- **Anchor Tent or Fly** by filling with sand or snow and burying it
- **Extract Water** by squeezing mud or lifting dew from vegetation
- **Filter Water** to remove dirt and sediment before drinking
- **First Starter** by collecting lint or tearing patch from socks
- **Harvest Small Game** by making a nun chuck to throw
- **Hold Hot Rocks** from fire to keep sleeping area warm
- **Improve Foot Grip** on ice by wearing over boots or shoes
- **Insulate** water bottles
- **Pad Clinking Items** in backpack to reduce noise
- **Pillow** by stuffing several socks into a bandana or a zip-tight plastic bag
- **Process Acorns** in a running stream to remove tannic acid
- **Protect Glass Bottles** in backpack
- **Protect Hands** when holding cookware over hot fire

- **Protect Raw or Hardboiled Eggs** in backpack
- **Shoulder Straps** or belt on an improvised backpack
- **Transport Things** like a sack tied around your belt
- **Warm Hands** by wearing like mittens
- **Wrap a Wound** to control bleeding or keep clean

Poncho

For dozens of alternative uses for a poncho, see these sections—earlier in this chapter.

- Tools: Mylar Blanket
- Tools: Trash Bags
- Tools: Tarps

Tools: Chapter Review

Chapter Summary

How will you remember all of this useful information?

- Mylar blankets, trash bags, tarps
- Cording, paracord, shock cord, rope, zip ties
- Duct tape, sunshade visor, cargo net
- Cattails for food, shelter, medicine, cordage, fire, and padding
- Plastic bottles, cooking oil, coffee filters, aluminum foil
- Sanitizer, glue, bandanas, hand warmers, floss, bags, and more!

Chapter Action Steps

☐ Save a copy of this information on your cell phone

☐ Update your backpack with some of the items in this chapter

☐ Test out some utilizations to ensure they work as expected

☐ How many plastic bottle projects can you do in a weekend?

☐ Impress a friend by sharing info in this chapter (or book)

☐ If you find this book useful, consider writing a brief review for it on Amazon.com. I'd also like to see your feedback for future books in this Prep Lists Books series. Thank you!

Plan to be spontaneous tomorrow. ☺

Next Chapter

Now you can do some amazing things with everyday tools that you may already have with you. To make the most of these tools, you will also need to practice some key skills, which are listed in the next chapter. You are quickly becoming an outdoor expert!

Chapter 6. Skills

Skills: Chapter Intro

You can have a pack full of expensive gear, you can be hiking through the most beautiful scenery, and you can have a heart that is full of good intentions. Many people set out thinking that these will be enough for a great trip, but they are not. You also need basic outdoor skills to deal with unexpected challenges and truly enjoy your adventure in the great outdoors.

A quick reminder: This is not an instruction manual.
This book is designed to give you information and ideas for action.

This chapter on skills includes the following topics.

Skills: Safety

Safety is always important. Safety always comes first. When making decisions away from home, keep safety in mind to avoid potential and unnecessary risks. Review these common issues to stay sharp.

- **Notification:** Always let someone know where you are and when you'll be back. Whether specific or just a vague guideline, when an emergency strikes, you'll be glad that you did. Consider also leaving a small note on your car just in case.
- **Maps:** Before setting out on a hike you should always do a quick refresher looking at a map of the surrounding area. It is best to have a backup map ready—whether on paper, on your cell phone, or even scratched on a napkin. Also, don't fully rely on GPS navigation—dead batteries, blocked reception, and more can become issues. I often take photographs of maps with my cell phone so that I can zoom into them without any reception.
- **Turn Back Time:** A common mistake for day hikers is first, not SETTING a turn back time, and then not TURNING AROUND at the pre-determined turn back time. Doing so risks being caught in the dark and spending the night cold and hungry.
- **After Dark:** Staying out after dark means you had better be prepared. To avoid it, know when sunset will be. Estimate it using your fingers between the sun and the horizon; each finger is about 1/4 hour of daylight. And you have a flashlight or headlamp, right?
- **Weather:** Always check the weather forecast to see if you need rain protection or extra clothing for warmth. Don't ignore signs that a storm is coming—get into a sheltered area before it hits. See **Chapter 4: Shelter** for more information.
- **Sunscreen:** Unless you already have a dark tan, you're going to need sunscreen or sunscreen spray. And don't wait until you have sunburn to start using it. Some sunscreens also include bug repellent.

- **First-Aid Kit:** Yes, taking this can be good, but don't overdo it. For most, a wallet-size kit is sufficient. Only take what you think you'd actually use and actually know how to use.
- **Water:** Don't assume that you'll find water along the trail. Plan on at least a gallon of water per person per day. See **Chapter 2: Water** for more information.
- **Group Speed:** Keep your group together. The first person sets a moderate pace to hold back speedsters. A sweeper follows behind. Agree to stop and regroup at every trail junction.
- **Shortcuts:** Avoid off-trail routes, especially if you're not familiar with the area. Doing so is just asking for trouble. Always stay in sight of recognizable landmarks if you need to leave the trail.
- **Backtracking:** When you have a wonderful loop planned for your hike, but somehow realize that you are lost... stop, turn around, and go back the way you came (especially if it's getting dark). Just decide that's what you wanted to do anyway.
- **Crossing Water:** Use extra caution when crossing streams & rivers. Rocks are slippery. Currents are strong. What is your backup plan if you get wet from head to toe? Don't take unnecessary risks.
- **Leaves:** Ascending or descending on wet or dry leaves can quickly take your feet out from under you. Tread carefully and always have a backup plan if you slip and fall—especially if a single foot slip could result in falling down a steep slope.
- **Fire:** If you plan to stay the night, always take multiple methods of starting a fire. See **Chapter 1: Fire** for more information.
- **Bear Bags:** Not just for bear, but all sorts of marauding varmints... if you are staying overnight, always keep your food (or anything that smells like food) out of reach—ideally tied up in a tree 100 yards downwind from your campsite.
- **Cell Phone:** While adding tremendous value to hiking safety when you need help, it's best to put your cell phone in a zip-tight plastic bag and forget that you even have it until there is an emergency. High ground usually offers better reception. Texting uses less battery power compared to voice or data. Most phones have built-in functions to save battery power.

Skills: Leave No Trace Ethics

"Leave No Trace" (LNT) is the name given to a set of outdoor ethics that promotes conservation of natural resources. The following principles are at the core of the LNT mindset.

Backcountry

- Plan ahead and prepare
- Travel and camp on durable surfaces
- Dispose of waste properly
- Leave what you find
- Minimize campfire impacts
- Respect wildlife
- Be considerate of other visitors

See It Online: LNT.org is the Center for Outdoor Ethics

Frontcountry

- Know before you go
- Stick to trails and camp overnight right
- Trash your trash and pick up poop
- Leave it as you find it
- Be careful with fire
- Keep wildlife wild
- Share our trails and manage your pet

See It Online: Wikipdeia.org – Leave No Trace

While there are many resources to guide you in great detail for proper methods in Leave No Trace (LNT) ethics, below is a sample from the state of Pennsylvania.

See It Online: Pennsylvania NCNR Forestry LNT

Plan Ahead and Prepare

- Know the regulations and special concerns for the area you'll visit.
- Prepare for extreme weather, hazards, and emergencies.
- Schedule your trip to avoid times of high use.
- Visit in small groups when possible. Consider splitting larger groups into smaller groups.
- Repackage food to minimize waste.
- Use a map and compass to eliminate the use of marking paint, rock cairns or flagging.

Travel and Camp on Durable Surfaces

- Durable surfaces include established trails and campsites, rock, gravel, dry grasses or snow.
- Protect riparian areas by camping at least 200 feet from lakes and streams.
- Good campsites are found, not made. Altering a site is not necessary.

In Popular Areas

- Concentrate use on existing trails and campsites.
- Walk single file in the middle of the trail, even when wet or muddy.
- Keep campsites small. Focus activity in areas where vegetation is absent.

In Pristine Areas

- Disperse use to prevent the creation of campsites and trails.
- Avoid places where impacts are just beginning.

Dispose of Waste Properly

- Pack it in, pack it out. Inspect your campsite and rest areas for trash or spilled foods. Pack out all trash, leftover food, and litter.
- Deposit solid human waste in catholes dug 6 to 8 inches deep at least 200 feet from water, camp, and trails. Cover and disguise the cathole when finished.
- Pack out toilet paper and hygiene products.
- To wash yourself or your dishes, carry water 200 feet away from streams or lakes and use small amounts of biodegradable soap. Scatter strained dishwater.

Leave What You Find

- Preserve the past: examine, but do not touch, cultural or historic structures and artifacts.
- Leave rocks, plants and other natural objects as you find them.
- Avoid introducing or transporting non-native species.
- Do not build structures, furniture, or dig trenches.

Minimize Campfire Impacts

- Campfires can cause lasting impacts to the backcountry. Use a lightweight stove for cooking and enjoy a candle lantern for light.
- Where fires are permitted, use established fire rings, fire pans, or mound fires.
- Keep fires small. Only use sticks from the ground that can be broken by hand.
- Burn all wood and coals to ash, put out campfires completely, then scatter cool ashes.

Respect Wildlife

- Observe wildlife from a distance. Do not follow or approach them.
- Never feed animals. Feeding wildlife damages their health, alters natural behaviors, and exposes them to predators and other dangers.
- Protect wildlife and your food by storing rations and trash securely.

- Control pets at all times, or leave them at home.
- Avoid wildlife during sensitive times: mating, nesting, raising young, or winter.

Be Considerate of Other Visitors

- Respect other visitors and protect the quality of their experience.
- Be courteous. Yield to other users on the trail.
- Step to the downhill side of the trail when encountering pack stock.
- Take breaks and camp away from trails and other visitors.
- Let nature's sounds prevail. Avoid loud voices and noises

Buy it Online: "Leave No Trace in the Outdoors" book by Jeffrey Marion

Skills: First Aid

Even when you have a kit or collection of first-aid supplies, you must also know how to use them—or how to improvise without them. Consider these topics to assess your personal preparedness. Perhaps this will motivate you to get additional training or do some reading on first aid skills.

Topics

Priorities

- Stop or prevent life-threatening dangers to yourself or others
- Project the injured person from any further harm
- Get medical help, if needed
- Treat life-threatening conditions first: breathing, beating, bleeding, bones

Breathing

- Choking
- Hyperventilation
- Stopped Breathing

Heartbeating

- Cardiopulmonary Resuscitation (CPR)
- Checking for pulse
- Heart Attack Warning Signals

Bleeding

- Arterial
- Nosebleed
- Skin Cuts
- Sterilizing
- Virus Protection

Bones

- Broken Collarbone
- Broken Finger
- Broken Limb

- Broken Ribs
- Broken Toe
- Head Injury
- Open Fracture
- Spinal Injury

Skin Wounds

- Bites & Stings
- Blisters
- Burns: First, Second, and Third-Degree
- Cuts and Scrapes
- Poisonous Plant Exposure
- Punctures or Fishhook
- Rash
- Splinter
- Sterilizing

Temperature

- Frost Bite
- Heat Exhaustion
- Heat Stroke
- Hypothermia

Other

- Asthma
- Dehydration
- Drowning
- Eye Injury
- Internal Poisoning
- Moving an injured or unconscious person
- Overdose
- Poisoning
- Seizures
- Shock
- Sprained Ankle
- Sunburn

Bad Advice

You may have heard these first aid myths. Now we know better. Educate yourself and help others to understand what to avoid.

- **Burns:** DO NOT treat with butter or oil.
- **Frostbite:** DO NOT rub skin to warm it.
- **Impaled:** DO NOT remove the object from the body.
- **Poisoned:** DO NOT add water or milk.
- **Poisoned:** DO NOT necessarily induce vomiting.
- **Seizures:** DO NOT place anything in mouth.
- **Snake Bite:** DO NOT try to suck out poison.

Assessments

- **Scene Survey:** Is it safe? What happened? How many victims? Can anyone help? Is anyone unconscious?
- **Primary Survey:** Ask if OK. Get consent to help. Check for ABCs—airway, breathing, and circulation.
- **Care for Shock:** Address cause of shock. Encourage rest. Keep warm. Give comfort.
- **Subjective Assessment:** SAMPLE: Signs, Allergies, Medications, Past medical history, Last meal, Events leading up to the emergency
- **Objective Assessment:** Level of consciousness, breathing, circulation, skin
- **Plan:** Identify the priority level and any needed actions

Learn more at RedCross.org

Sampling of Basic First Aid Skills

- **Abdominal Thrusts** for choking baby
- **Bleeding Control** to stop bleeding and prevent infection
- **Cooling Down** a victim of heat stroke (hot skin)
- **Cooling Off** a victim of heat exhaustion (cold skin)
- **CPR** for stopped heart and breathing
- **Epi-Pen Use** for anaphylaxis or severe allergy
- **Heimlich Maneuver** for choking

- **Low Blood Sugar** Treatment
- **Tourniquets** to properly stop major hemorrhaging
- **Treating** a victim for shock
- **Warming Up** a victim of Hypothermia
- **>>> Calling for Help <<<**

Getting Help

- Dial 911
- Have local police or emergency phone numbers
- Have emergency contact numbers, like spouse or parent
- Have poison center number: 1-800-764-7661

Know what to communicate when you call...

- Victim location
- Injury or illness description of victim
- Amount of time that has passed since issue started
- Treatment already given to victim
- What extra equipment might be needed (stretcher, food, water, shelter, warm clothing, etc.)

Skills: Navigation

If you've never gotten lost, don't worry, someday you likely will. It has happened to just about everyone. The key is knowing what to do when you realize it has happened to you. There are also skills to help keep you on track as you head toward your destination. Consider these navigational abilities.

Tools

Know how to use these navigational tools.

- Maps (paper, electronic, photographs, topo, etc.)
- GPS (dedicated device or cell phone app)
- Compass (magnetic, shadow, or improvised)
- Eyes (observe landmarks and patterns)

General Strategies

- **Plan Ahead:** Know the route—and any alternate routes—before you leave. Look at it on a map. Draw yourself a map. Know in your head where you are at all times.
- **Topo Maps:** Use the topographic features to create a mental picture of hills, valleys, streams, trails, and mountain ridges.
- **Pay Attention:** Remember to notice unique landmarks, take note of consistent patterns like streams, ridges, tree lines, or sun direction. Keep a mental map in your head so you can backtrack.
- **Practice Mental Mapping:** Try going on a new trail—maybe with a partner who's been there before, and when your hike is finished, draw a map of where you were. Then compare your map to a real map or satellite image and see how accurate you were.
- **Keep Your Bearings:** Look around every once in a while and estimate which way is north and know what direction you're headed. This will help avoid going in circles—which sounds too silly to be true but it really does happen. Keep a mental map in your head for where you started, where you are, and where you're going.

- **Timestamps:** Whenever you pass a landmark or milestone, make a quick note of the time so you can estimate how long it will take to return to that point.
- **Think Logically:** If you think you might be lost, before rushing in a new direction, sit down and think about it. Review the recent milestones and landmarks in your head—especially if you have a map to study. Give yourself time to solve the problem. Usually backtracking is better than taking a new shortcut.
- **Perspective:** If you're not sure where you are, consider getting to a higher point to better see what is around you. Remember things that are consistent, like water always flows downhill, the sun always moves from east to west, and the prevailing wind is usually from the same direction.
- **GPS Dependent:** Know how to navigate even if your GPS fails or loses power.

Orienteering

If you want to get serious about using your compass and map to navigate, learn more (or refresh your memory) about this common terminology and jargon.

- Aiming-Off
- Aspect of Slope
- Attack Point
- Bearing
- Back Bearing
- Contour
- Draw
- Features: Catching, Fathering, Line, Tick
- Hand Railing
- Heading
- Saddle
- Target

Estimating Measurements

Use navigational and geometry skills to estimate measurements.

- **Measuring Distance:** (Field) Pacing or striding a sample area
- **Measuring Height:** (Tree) Stick or felling methods
- **Measuring Widths:** (Stream) Salute, stick, or compass methods
- **Measuring Time:** Counting, sun, or stars methods
- **Measuring Level:** Water bottle

Finding North

Use any of these methods to determine which direction is north, and then proceed in the desired direction.

Magnetic Compass

This inexpensive device comes in many shapes and sizes, quickly and easily pointing toward the earth's magnetic north pole. Be sure that you really know how to use it—and how to avoid magnetic interference. You can also make your own with a sewing needle and a container of water.

Remember that where you live determines the accuracy of magnetic north vs. true north. Across the United States, there is a 40 degree variance.

Shadow Compass

This method will require at least half an hour of sun (or moon) observation. Place a long stick vertically into the ground. Mark the end of the shadow created by the stick. Repeat every 15 minutes to see the direction of the sun (or moon). The line created by your markers is a rough east/west line, with the shadow moving from west to east.

Analog Watch

Set your watch, or a replica of a watch, to the current time without the daylight saving adjustment. Hold the watch flat and aim the hour hand toward the sun. Imagine a line half way between the hour hand and 12 o'clock on your watch. This line points north.

Nighttime Stars

Find the Big Dipper constellation. Use the last two stars of the front of the bucket that line up with the North Star. Point to the North Star and you are pointing north.

Skills: Signaling

When you need help, being able to communicate your need to potential rescuers is critical. Perhaps most important is making yourself visible from both the ground and from the air, so that rescuers can find you. Remember that a standard, international distress signal is three short blasts—of sound, light, or any signal. You can also use three signals in the shape of a triangle—like three smoking campfires.

Nearby

- Headlamp or flashlight (at night)
- Whistle
- Voice (scream and yell): Only if you can hear others
- Gunfire
- Banging sticks or metal plates
- Loudly blaring radio

Distant

- **Mirror with sunlight:** or a reflective watch, a spoon, a compact disc or DVD, the bottom of an aluminum can, or cut it open to expose the shiny interior of the aluminum can
- **Fire by night:** Tall and bright
- **Fire with smoke by day:** Use evergreen boughs for smoke
- **High-contrast colors and movement:** Like waving an orange jacket on a stick like a flag
- **Brightly colored** tarp, tent, or blanket

Morse Code for "SOS" is "dit-dit-dit, dah-dah-dah, dit-dit-dit" or ••• – – – •••

Direction

Let others know where you've been and where you're going.

- Tie small strands of cloth, paper, or string to tree branches
- Drop pieces of brightly colored paper
- Make cairns of rocks
- Break and bend over tall weeds, tree limbs, or small trees

Skills: Survival

An entire book could be written about survival skills. In fact, it is being planned as a future book in the Prep Lists Books series.

For this context, consider the following checklist of survival skills that you may want to explore further.

- Bartering Skills and Supplies
- Blacksmithing
- Boats and Rafts
- Bushcraft and Campcraft
- Caching Supplies
- Camouflage
- Climbing and Rappelling
- Cold Weather Proficiencies
- Cooking Basics with Limited Resources
- Edible Plant Identification
- Fire Starting and Fire Building
- Firearms for Defense
- Firearms for Hunting
- First Aid and CPR
- Fishing
- Foods Preservation and Storage
- Gardening and Sprouting Seeds
- Homesteading
- Hunting
- Hygiene in the Field
- Knife Uses and Knife Sharpening
- Knots and Lashings
- Leather Tanning
- Lighting Improvising
- Livestock Raising
- Medicinal Plant Identification
- Mental Conditioning
- Orienteering with Maps and Compass
- Physical Conditioning

- Pioneering
- Primitive Weapons for Hunting
- Processing Small and Large Game
- Rope and Cordage Making
- Self-Defense
- Self-Reliance
- Signaling and Communications
- Snowshoes and Skis
- Spiritual and Emotional Health
- Swimming
- Tool Improvising
- Tracks and Tracking
- Trapping and Snaring
- Tree Felling with Axe or Saw
- Water Sourcing, Transporting, and Purifying
- Weapons for Self Defense

Skills: Knot Tying

Tying knots is an essential skill in the outdoors. Always have some cording available and remember to regularly practice a handful of basic knots—knowing when and why to use each—so that you will have confidence that your knots will hold properly. The following list of knots will address most situations.

See the Tools: Cording section in Chapter 5 for related information.

Knots

Here are some common knots to know before you go.

- **Bowline:** Used around someone's waist for rescue, this large loop holds tight without slipping or cinching, and can be tied quickly

The way I remember how to tie a bowline knot is the story of the snake that comes out of a hole, goes around the tree, and then goes back down the hole.

- **Clove Hitch:** Used to attach a rope to a pole or tree, may be used to start Bushcraft lashing projects
- **Figure 8 Stopper:** Used next to another knot to prevent it from slipping
- **Sheepshank:** Used to shorten a rope or to work around a weak spot in the rope
- **Sheet Bend:** Used to join two ropes, or two handkerchiefs, or two sheets; especially useful when the two items are different sizes
- **Square (Reef) Knot:** Used for non-load-bearing cording, quick and easy to tie and untie, but susceptible to breaking the rope under strain
- **Taut Line Hitch:** Used to adjust tension, like tightening a guy line between a tent and a stake.
- **Two Half Hitches:** Used to attach a rope to a pole with greater security

Bonus: Practice these knots until you can do them with your eyes closed… or in the dark with cold fingers during a windy rainstorm.

Knot Terminology

Understanding these terms will help when learning new knots and applying their advantages.

- **Running End:** Also Working End—used to tie the knot
- **Standing Part:** The opposite end from the running end
- **Dressing:** Adjusting a knot into proper position
- **Bight:** Doubling back in a U shape, without forming a loop
- **Overhand Loop:** When the running end is on top
- **Underhand Loop:** When the running end is on the bottom
- **Hitch:** A knot attaching rope to an object
- **Turn:** Wrapping the rope around an object and continuing
- **Roundturn:** Wrapping the rope around an object and returning

Skills: Bush Craft

While bush craft takes many forms, it is generally using cording and natural materials—like sticks and logs—to create useful objects when camping. Sometimes other materials like a tarp or blanket may also be used. The essential skill for bush craft is lashing—the binding of two or more poles together with rope or cording. There are many bush craft books available for various projects with detailed instructions and illustrations. Here are just a few ideas to consider or for future investigation.

Sample Bush Craft Projects

- **Backpack:** A rough frame with tarp, blanket, trash bag, etc.
- **Basket:** Weave reeds, bark, grass, etc. into a useful container
- **Bridge:** Lash poles, logs, and ropes together to cross a stream
- **Bucksaw:** Build around a bow saw blade for cutting larger logs (The blade by itself is very small and lightweight in a backpack)
- **Camera Stand:** Rigging to hold cell phone or camera in tree for taking selfies, videos, or time-lapse photography
- **Camp Chair:** An A-Frame leaning against a tree
- **Campfire Reflector:** A wall of logs, maybe with Mylar blanket
- **Firewood Luggage:** Two sticks and two ropes to carry several armfuls of firewood in a single trip
- **Fish Hook:** Made from locust thorn or toothpick-like wedge
- **Frogging Gig:** A four-pronged spear with barbs
- **Platform:** Lash many poles together for a raised floor or table
- **Raft:** Last layers of small logs together to float downstream
- **Rake:** Used to clear area for campfire or pile up leaves and duff under sleeping area
- **Reclining Chair:** Hang a jacket or blanket from a tripod
- **Tent Stakes:** T-shaped or Y-shaped to hold rope and pull easily
- **Tent:** Any A-Frame structure to keep the rain and snow off
- **Tree Chair:** Hang a jacket or blanket from an A-Frame
- **Water Bottle Tongs:** Forked branch to lift hot from fire

Do you have ideas for more bush craft projects in a future book? Please visit PrepListsBooks.com and use the Feedback Form to tell me more.

Skills: Heat

Being able to create or retain heat is very useful… and doesn't always mean building a campfire. Here are a few examples to consider.

Purposes for Heat

- Cooking food
- Warming food
- Making hot drinks
- Purifying water for drinking
- Keeping body and skin warm
- Creating a comfortable environment like a tent or hammock

*See the **Sleeping Warm** section in Chapter 4 for more information.*

Sources of Heat

- Campfire (convection and radiation), stove, lantern, fire containers, rocks warmed in a fire, the sun's solar radiation, geothermal, vehicle, friction, hand warmers, portable heaters, exercise, technology…

Fuels to Product Heat

- Wood, alcohol, alcogel, propane, natural gas, coal, oil, chemical combinations, food for your own body heat

*See the Weather Preparation > **Cold Days** section in this chapter for more information.*

Skills: Light

Producing light is very useful at night... and doesn't always mean building a campfire. Here are a few ideas to consider.

Fire

- Campfire
- Torch
- Tiki Light
- Lamp
- Signal Fire

Lanterns

It's best to know what type of lantern fits your needs.

- **Butane:** Common, safe, best when above 40 degrees Fahrenheit
- **Gas:** Bright, open flame hazard, more expensive
- **Kerosene:** Heavy and durable
- **Propane:** Canisters of propane are easy to find and often interchangeable with other devices used for heating and cooking
- **Electric:** Various models, lightweight, safe, duration varies

Flashlights

With so many available, you'll need to understand what type of flashlight is best for your situation.

Headlamps

Many people are switching from flashlights to headlamps. Do you know the value of each?

Skills: Bug Protection

The tiniest of creatures can ruin a great adventure in the outdoors, so always remember to take some sort of bug repellent. While most bugs are just a nuisance, others present a real threat—like biting ants and disease-carrying ticks. So be prepared and know what products are safe for skin, safe for kids, safe for food, and more!

If small bugs are buzzing around your face,
try raising your hand to see if the fly around your hand instead.

Bugs: Sprays

- Permethrin: This is one of the best (and more expensive) products at killing bugs like ticks, chiggers, and mosquitos on contact, preventing them from landing on or climbing through treated clothing, but it is not as effective at keeping them from buzzing around your face or landing on your skin. Spray Permethrin on hats, pants, shirts, sleeping bag, tent, and more. It should last in fabric through half a dozen wash cycles.
- OFF! Deep Woods Insect Repellent: This has been very effective on many of my camping trips.
- Repel Natural Insect Repellent: This is a great product, especially if you need to be DEET-free.

Repellents with DEET may melt nylon, polyester, plastics, and water bladders.
So be sure to keep in a zip-tight plastic bag in case it leaks.

Bugs: Wipes

- Bug Wipes are a great alternative to sprays for quick and easy application to skin, clothing, or other objects.
- Dryer Sheets: Rub on skin, clothing, or keep under hat

Bugs: Wearables

- Sawyer Products Permethrin for clothing
- There are many ultrasonic repellent devices that work well
- Hang a personal clip-on mosquito repellent on you or in your tent; it uses AAA batteries and works wonders to keep the mosquitos away. Refills last 12 hours.
- Thermacell mosquito-repellant wearable devices

- Wearing bug repellent bracelets is a nice alternative to applying chemicals to your skin. Here are a few brands that work well.
  > Cliganic Natural Mosquito Repellent Bracelet, Waterproof
  > STURME 20 Pack Natural Mosquito Repellent Bracelets, Waterproof, Bug Insect Protection up to 300 Hours, No DEET
  > Original Kinven Mosquito Insect Repellent Bracelet, Waterproof, Natural, DEET FREE, Anti Mosquito Protection

Tip: Wear light-colored clothing, because mosquitos are attracted to dark colors

Bugs: Tent & Campsite

- Thermacell mosquito-repellant bug-free zone devices
- Keep tent door facing the wind; bugs like to hover downwind from wind blocks like your tent
- Smoke from a campfire deters many bugs and mosquitos
- Adding sage to your campfire keeps mosquitos and bugs away
- Keep attended campfire going 24/7 to push bugs back

Bugs: Home Products

To repel bugs using scent, try using these everyday items that you may already have at home.

- Avon Skin-So-Soft lotion or sunscreen
- Baby Powder repels bees and wasps on children's skin
- Basil
- Bay leaves
- Bounce dryer sheets repel yellow jacket wasps
- Cinnamon
- Citronella
- Fairy Tales Rosemary Repel shampoo, gel, spray
- Garlic—eating or wearing
- Lemon Eucalyptus Oil
- Rosemary
- Rub the inside of an orange peel on face and any exposed skin
- Tea tree oil (by itself or in other products)
- White Vinegar: on clothing, tent, backpack to repel ants

Bugs: Avoid

- Avoid perfumes or colognes that smell sweet or fruity
- Avoid dark clothing, which attracts mosquitos
- Avoid food or drink in tent that may attract bugs
- Avoid pitching tent near standing water or beneath trees
- Avoid unnecessary lights that attract bugs
- Avoid keep bags of trash nearby (burn or remove)
- Avoid unwashed cooking gear left out

Many bugs, like mosquitos, are drawn to the carbon dioxide in your breath. Controlled breathing, or staying in a breeze, helps keep them out of your face.

Bugs: Ticks

If you are in an area prone to ticks, consider these tips.

- Avoid brushing up against tall grass, bushes, trees, etc.
- Spray shoes & pants with 1 part tea tree oil and 2 parts water
- Tuck in shirt & pant cuffs
- Check yourself regularly
- Every 24 hours, do a full body exam (like when showering)
- Remember that ticks cannot pass Lyme disease to you in the first 24 hours they are attached to you. Just remove and sterilize.

Bugs: Pets

- Remember to use bug repellent for dogs, too.
- Springtime "Bug Off Garlic Chewables for Dogs" (and horses) is very effective

Skills: Toilet Time

Eventually it's going to happen, no matter how much you prepare. You'll need to either urinate or poop in the woods without a toilet in sight. Consider these ideas to make the job easier.

Tools

- Remember to keep some form of toilet paper (TP) with you
- Keep your TP in a zip-tight plastic bag to keep it dry
- Prep pre-sized lengths so you can quickly grab with one hand
- Consider travel tissue packs that come in re-sealable bags
- Consider pre-cut portions of heavy-duty paper towels instead of long rolls of fluffy TP.
- TP makes a useful barter item on the trail (think value vs. weight)
- **Toilet Paper Alternatives:** If you have no toilet paper, consider these alternatives: smooth rocks, green leaves (non-poisonous), green pine cones, smooth-barked branches, moss, corn husks, dried corn cobs, coffee filters, napkins, handkerchief, rags, towels, cut off shirt tail, socks, pages of a book, paper bag, dollar bills, snow, stream water, etc.
- **TP Efficiency:** First wipe with natural alternatives (listed above), and then finish with a minimum amount of soft toilet paper.

Tips

- Remember that no matter how remote you are, others will follow. Be considerate and completely cover or bury your waste.
- Leave No Trace (LNT) principles suggest going at least 200 feet from trail, water, or campsite.
- Ideally, find a spot with soft dirt covered by thick layer of leaves and duff. First, remove the top layer (leaves) and set aside to cover (hide) when you are finished.
- Dig a hole in soft dirt with whatever is handy: shovel, trowel, heavy stick, bundle of small sticks, rock, heel of boot, hands, etc. Six to eight inches deep should be good. Pile up dirt removed from hole for easy burial and cover.

If camping in the winter with frozen ground, do not think that burying your waste in the snow is sufficient. Pack it out in zip-tight plastic bags. A waste kit or WAG Bag can help, which may include sanitizer, neutralizer, and more. Bonus: use snow to wipe instead of toilet paper.

- Take care of your toilet paper (based on your location and commitment to LNT): bury it, burn/bury it, or pack it out.

Consider these popular pooping positions.

- **Squatting:** Quick and easy, just be sure to miss your pants
- **Leaning:** Put your back or butt up against something solid like a tree or rock
- **Hanging:** Holding on to nearby branches is especially helpful when weighted down with heavy gear or over-clothes
- **Sitting:** Ideal if you can find the perfect set of logs or branches, shaped like a toilet seat

Cautions

- Avoid baring skin to snakes, spiders, ticks, and other insects.
- Avoid touching (or wiping with) poison ivy, poison oak, etc.
- Avoid getting scratched in thorny briars.
- Avoid getting your clothes, suspenders, coat, gear, etc. soiled.
- Avoid diaper rash: always use something to clean yourself.

Remember to wash your hands when finished.
Use hand sanitizer if that's all you have.

Periods

Don't let that time of the month prevent you from enjoying a trip to the great outdoors.

- It's a myth that menstrual blood attracts bear. It does not.
- Have a kit ready to keep your supplies clean, dry, and organized
- Learn menstrual options for tampon/pad vs. a re-usable cup

Skills: Weather Preparation

Think about how the weather is going to affect your time outdoors.

- **Unseasonably warm or cold?** Ideal clothing and bedding?
- **Unexpected rain or snow?** Proper shelter and footwear?
- **Severe thunderstorms and lightning?** Think safety first
- **Potential flooding?** Know where you are and where to go
- **A change in the weather?** Alternate plans or activities?

These topics and more are in the following sections.

Rain

When thinking about camping, hiking, and backpacking, you probably imagine clear skies and beautiful weather. But, eventually, it will rain. If you are prepared, you can still enjoy your time outdoors—even when it is raining.

Key Principles for Rain

- Wet = Cold
- Keep head dry; keep feet dry—especially when sleeping
- Keep gear dry; if wet, dry out as soon as you are able
- Avoid sweating under rain gear
- Keep wet things out of your sleeping area
- Use talcum powder or cornstarch to dry wet skin

Remember that rain makes rocks very slippery

Prep for Rain

Before you leave home...

- Keep clothing in a waterproof bag or container
- Take extra waterproof zip-tight plastic bags for wet clothing
- Use heavy-duty compactor trash bags to line pack or boots
- Test your rain gear to ensure it works as expected
- Use a dry bag/box for your electronics & fire starters
- Take food that does not require cooking or a campfire
- Review the weather forecast and plan accordingly
- Re-waterproof your boots if it's been a while

Before the rain starts...

- Set up tent/shelter and protect gear
- Collect and cover firewood with tarp or evergreen branches
- Have rain clothing ready to put on
- Use extra tarps over and under to keep rainwater out
- Position tent & campfire away from low areas collecting water
- Camp on high ground, avoiding any chance of flooding

Remember that most waterproof clothing is 100% effective at retaining sweat. :-)

Gear for Rain

- Hat: wide brim keeps rain off, or use a billed cap under hood
- Umbrella: collapsible, packable, versatile, moving or stationary
- Jacket/Shell: lightweight, pockets, hooded, waterproof
- Poncho: cheap plastic/vinyl, or durable nylon, best without wind
- Rain Pants: waterproof, best for heavy rain and wet terrain
- Boots: waterproof material/treatment, high water line, good grip
- Gaiters: keep feet and footwear dry and protected
- Pack Cover: if poncho doesn't cover pack, or for use in camp
- Waterproof Stuff Sacks: usually better than leaky pack covers
- Paracord: Use as a clothesline to dry out your clothes and gear
- Lots of plastic bags: to keep things dry or put wet things in

If you see lightning or hear thunder, avoid being in water and avoid high points like ridges.

Improvised Rain Protection

- Use any garbage bag for poncho, pack cover, or wet clothing
- A huge 95-gallon trash bag can be used as a sleeping bag wrapper, Bivy, full-length poncho, shelter roof, and more.
- Consider a large tarp canopy high over your entire campsite
- Newspaper can be used to start fires when everything else is wet, to help dry out the inside of your shoes overnight
- Collect rain water for drinking water to keep a full supply
- A spray can of Camp Dry Water Repellent can make most any fabric water resistant

Snow

There are great advantages to camping, hiking, or backpacking when there's snow on the ground—no annoying insects, no biting reptiles, not as many people, and the splendid beauty of the season. There's nothing quite like a hot drink by a cozy fire on a chilly night. Along with this comes additional planning to deal with the raw elements of winter.

Prepared people love winter camping.
Unprepared people hate winter camping.

Key Principles for Snow

- **Snow melts into water:** project your bedding, gear, campfire
- **Snow hides things:** gear, trails, landmarks
- **Snow adds weight:** remove buildup as needed
- **Snow may freeze things in place:** especially melt & re-freeze
- **Snow may indicate frozen earth beneath it:** driving stakes
- **Snow is a fire inhibitor:** can be good or bad
- **Snow melted is drinkable:** boil over fire before drinking

See also: the Sleeping Warm section in Chapter 4.

Prep for Snow

Consider these to deal with snow in your campsite.

- A compass and map may help if your usual hiking trails are covered and hidden by snow
- Avoid setting up camp under trees that are covered with snow that may fall during a windy night
- Angled tarp over tent or hammock to keep falling snow off
- Snow tent pegs, stakes, and guy lines (bury in snow rather than digging into frozen earth)
- Groundsheet under tent, hammock, etc. to keep your gear and footwear dry
- Pack down snow under your tent before setting up to make sleeping more comfortable
- If it is windy, dig or build a snow wall to block or avoid wind

- Bring a piece of corrugated cardboard or a car visor shade to stand on when you're changing your clothes or boots
- With the increased risks related to camping with snow, be sure someone knows where you are and have reliable communication with civilization if you need help

Remember that if you leave your car to camp in the snow, you will need to get the car back out onto the road; so park in a way that makes that easier, and have good shovel ready.

Gear for Snow

Consider which of these might be useful on your trip.

- **Boots**: These may be higher and more waterproof than usual
- **Crampons**: Walking on ice
- **Cross Country Skis**: Faster than plodding through snow
- **Gaiters**: Keep snow out of your boots
- **Ice Axe**: Climbing rock faces
- **Lip Balm**: Wind and cold make for sore, chapped lips
- **Shovel**: Foldable, lightweight, use to clear out campsite
- **Snow Saw**: Making bricks for shelter
- **Snowshoes**: Trudging through deep snow
- **Sunscreen**: Yes, you can get sunburnt in a snowfield
- **Thermometer**: Know when it is above or below 32 degrees, when water will freeze or melt
- **Toboggan or Sled**: Transporting heavy gear over snow
- **Trekking Poles**: For skis, snowshoes, balance, or knee support

Improvised Snow

- Shovel out, mound up, or stack up snow as part of your shelter
- Use snow as a wind block
- Pile snow around your tent as insulation and reduce drafts
- Use snow under bedding to insulate you from the frozen ground
- Dig a trench in the snow for your feet so you can sit on one side and cook or eat on the other side
- Dig hole in front of tent to make getting in and out easier.
- Fill plastic grocery bags with snow and bury for tent anchors

Remember that your speed of travel will likely be slower in snow.

Cold Days

To stay warm in cold weather, consider the following.

Key Principles for Cold

- Keep out of the wind
- Keep your head, wrists, and ankles covered
- A warm hat can help retain nearly half of your body heat
- Adjusting layers of clothing keeps you comfortable when active
- Avoid sweating, which will make you very cold when resting
- Clothing loses its insulating ability when wet or dirty
- Try to always eat hot, hearty meals rather than just cold snacks
- Prep meals at home to minimize time with bare, wet fingers exposed to the cold air
- Cold toes may indicate boot laces that are too tight

See also: the Sleeping Warm section in Chapter 4.

Prep for Cold

- **Layers:** Better than a single coat for warmth, wear several layers that can be added and removed as needed
- **Layers:** Shed layers of clothing as soon as you start to sweat
- **Synthetics:** Avoid Cotton clothing and wear synthetics instead
- **Calories:** You will need to eat more calories for warmth, so take more fats and proteins instead of just carbohydrates
- **Pot of Water:** Fill cooking/coffee pot with water before going to sleep at night, since you can't pour frozen water
- **Water Bottle:** Hang upside down so ice forms from bottom up
- **A hot drink** can warm your body and your spirits
- **Create a wind barrier** using a tarp, trees, snow, clothing, etc.
- **Use a heavier sleeping bag** or extra liners, like fleece or flannel
- **Use an extra sleeping pad** to insulate from the frozen ground
- **Moisture:** Don't sleep with your face in your sleeping bag; the moisture in your breath will make you colder
- **Lips:** Wear plenty of lip balm (or Vaseline) when you sleep
- **Drying:** Quickly dry out your sleeping bag by turning it inside out and draping it over your tent or tree branches

Gear for Cold

Beyond the obvious warm clothing, consider these ideas.

- **Scarf**: Anything wrapped around your neck or head will help keep your entire body much warmer
- **Hat**: A hat keeps your whole body warm, including your feet.
- **Extra Socks**: Keep feet dry and switch socks when they get wet
- **Thermometer**: Know when it is above or below 32 degrees, when water will freeze or melt
- **Heat Packs**: Either chemical, combustible, or other types of hand and foot warmers
- **Folded Saw**: This type of folding hand saw is my preferred wood cutter in my backpack. Lightweight, strong, and portable, it's a reliable method of quickly collecting dry firewood.
- **Pocket Chain Saw**: These pocket chain saws come in various sizes, weights, and strengths. The key for long-term use is keeping the chain straight when cutting.
- **Hands**: Wear latex or nitrile exam gloves as glove liners

Improvised for Cold

- **Yoga mats** can also be used as an insulating sleeping pad
- **Extra Layer of Insulation:** Use Car Reflector Visors by binding edges together with zip ties, twist ties, cording, or thread to create sleeping pad or sleeping bag liner
- **Backpack Foot Box:** Use your backpack or zipped-up coat as a foot cover for extra insulation while sleeping
- **Socked Water Bottles:** Wrap water bottles in thick socks (and other clothing) to keep from freezing as quickly
- **Sleeping Pad:** Sit on pad during the day to keep bum warm
- **Zipper Pulls:** Tie loops of cording around zipper pulls to make them easier when wearing gloves or mittens
- **Oven Bags:** Wear heavy-duty plastic bags like oven bags between your socks and boots to keep boots dry, or under socks to keep socks dry.
- **Ice Melt:** Make your own hand warmers with zip-tight plastic bags and ice melt pellets. Just add water to create heat.

Hot Days

To stay cooler in hot weather, these tips may be helpful.

No power cords are needed for these low-tech tips.

Key Principles

- You need water to cope with heat
- Your body sweats to cool down by evaporation
- Encourage sweat evaporation with a breeze (moving air)
- Moisten skin to encourage cooling evaporation
- Sweating uses water that needs to be replaced by drinking
- Caffeinated drinks pull water out of your body

See also: the Sleeping Cool section in Chapter 4.

Prep for Heat

Clothing…

- **Wear a wet bandana** around neck or forehead to cool full body
- **Wear lightweight, loose-fitting, light-colored, synthetic clothing** that breathes to stay dry. If you tend toward dehydration then maybe wear Cotton to keep skin damp.
- **Wear a hat** to keep direct sunlight off your head and face
- **Wear sandals** or flip flops instead of boots around camp
- **Use or make an umbrella** that keeps the sun off your head

Whenever you pass water, soak your shirt, hat, or bandana.
If you have a spare, get it wet and keep it in a zip-tight plastic bag to wear later.

Skin…

- **Prepare bug deterrents** so you can expose more of your skin
- **Use plenty of lip balm** to keep lips from drying & chapping
- **Remember the sunblock** lotion or sunscreen spray

Food…

- **Take food that does not require cooking** or a campfire
- **Use the Sun:** Cook with a solar oven instead of a campfire
- **Freeze a small cooler** in a freezer or larger cooler to last longer
- **Make ice blocks** by freezing water jugs and drink when melted

- **Ice packs** can be strategically placed for extended life
- **Large ice blocks** last longer than bags of ice cubes
- **Use two coolers:** the one with drinks gets opened frequently, the one with food stays shut to last longer
- **Avoid opening coolers** too often so they stay cold longer

Location...

- **Choose a campsite with afternoon shade** (trees to the west)
- **Camp near water**, especially near moving water
- **Air around a rippling brook** will be cooler
- **A campsite near a slope** or hillside has more air movement
- **Remove the tent rain fly** if it's not raining
- **Protect tent from sun:** Drape a reflective space blanket over it
- **Stay in the shade** and avoid direct sunlight when possible
- **Create shade** by hanging a tarp or sleeping bag like an awning
- **Allow the air to move** over you whenever possible
- **Water:** Know where & how to get plenty of safe drinking water
- **Caves and rock outcroppings** may provide cooler air

Activities...

- **Avoid midday activities** when the sun is hottest
- **Schedule activities** for early morning or evening when coolest
- **Get wet to cool off** during the heat of the day
- **Use a misting system** (or spray bottle) for evaporation cooling

Sleeping...

- **Use an appropriate sleeping bag** for the temperature
- **Lightweight sheets** are cooler than a sleeping bag
- **Skip the tent** and just take a Bivy or rainfly in case of rain
- **Hammock sleeping** in a breeze is much cooler than a tent
- **Cot:** Sleeping on a Mesh Cot with circulating air helps stay cool
- **Line up your tent with the prevailing wind** to keep it aired out
- **Wear wet socks to bed**, especially if exposed to a breeze

Dark Nights

Don't laugh! If you've ever arrived at the planned campsite later than expected and had to deal with setting up a tent, unpacking your backpack, or looking for firewood in the dark, then you understand the importance of this topic.

Key Principles for Darkness

- **Best Advice:** Start setting up camp one to two hours before sunset to avoid dealing with darkness
- **Ambient Light:** If there is any starlight or moonlight, it may be better to let your eyes adjust to the dim light rather than struggling with limited artificial light like a flashlight

Priorities for Darkness

If it is almost dark when you start making camp, consider working on these priorities first.

- Determine where everything will be, like tent, hammock, campfire, firewood, cooking area, gear, trash, latrine, etc.
- Make sure everyone in the group knows where things should go and divide the responsibilities
- Collect firewood that is further from campsite first; stumbling through the woods in the dark is like asking for trouble
- Make a rough pile of firewood without taking time to break it down, cut it up, or sort it out
- Build a tall (not large) campfire to light the other activities

Be extremely careful using any sort of open flame for light, which can very quickly become a forest fire hazard.

Prep for Darkness

- **Cell Phone:** Learn how to turn your phone into a bright flashlight using the camera's flash—either in the phone settings or as an app
- **Cell Phone:** Find a bright white screen on your cell phone for moderate light and less battery consumption
- **Batteries:** If you have any sort of electronic illumination—flashlight, lantern, cell phone... you'll eventually need batteries.

- **Candles:** If you can use candles safely, these are very helpful

Gear for Darkness

- **Flashlight:** Flashlights have various sizes, shapes, brightness, weight, longevity, battery efficiency, and many more options
- **Headlamp:** These head-mounted flashlights are best to keep both of your hands free for working and carrying things
- **Lantern:** Lantern lights use various fuel for basic illumination inside a tent or blinding light that fills the entire campsite

If a tree falls in the forest and no one is around to see it,
do the other trees make fun of it?

Skills: Oops

Plan ahead to avoid these camping and backpacking problems.

- **Protect bug spray:** Keep in zip-tight plastic bags; Deet bug repellent sprays melt nylon, polyester, some plastics, and some water bladders
- **Set a turn back time:** Even if you don't reach your hiking destination goal, know when to turn around so you can get back before dark
- **Organize your backpack:** Keep things you'll need quickly or regularly on top or in a side pocket
- **Dress appropriately for the weather:** Know the weather forecast and wear sufficient clothing and footwear; taking off layers as needed
- **Start cool:** When you first start your hike, you should feel a little cool, so you don't get sweaty and need to change clothes just a few minutes later
- **Keep drinking water from freezing:** pack your water bottles upside down so that if they start to freeze, you can still drink from them.
- **"Start as a group, hike as a group, finish as a group."** This is good advice to avoid major problems for everyone if there's a wrong turn, an injury or sickness, or if a sudden storm hits
- **Avoid backpack danglers:** Keep your gear inside or strapped tightly, not swinging loosely—catching on trees and bushes, making noise, throwing you off balance
- **Wear your sunscreen:** It's not enough to have sunscreen after your skin starts burning; wear it to protect yourself and keep your skin happy—even on cloudy days
- **Don't burn bridges:** When hiking, climbing, or descending rocky trails, be sure you can always return the way you came
- **Use the switchbacks:** Unless there is deep snow, hiking the greater distance uphill back and forth through switchbacks takes less energy than climbing a straight line up the steep slope

- **Use multiple layers of rain projection:** Instead of relying on a single pack cover that is prone to leaking, keep your gear in a waterproof stuff sack, and important things like electronics in additional waterproof, zip-tight plastic bags

Skills: Balance

Ultralight vs. Ultra-heavy... camping and backpacking is often a balance between taking too many unnecessary luxuries and lacking key essentials when you need them most. Consider the following to find your personal zone for optimal balance.

- Batteries: fresh set vs. extra backup set
- Bulky clothing vs. layered clothing
- Clothing options
- Cookware vs. sticks or just water
- Durability vs. lightweight vs. space-saving
- Eating cold food vs. heating and cooking
- First-Aid Kit and Repair Kit vs. small bag with essentials only
- Food: calorie-dense vs. variety and flavorful
- Pack type
- Rain gear vs. backup trash bag
- Reliability vs. efficiency
- Replace old gear with newer, lighter, smaller gear
- Safety vs. weight
- Sleeping bag type: comfort vs. size vs. weight vs. warmth
- Tarp ground sheets vs. Tyvek sheets (lighter and stronger)
- Tarps vs. Rainflies (lighter, smaller, and more expensive)
- Tent vs. hammock vs. Bivy
- Too many backups
- Too much stuff
- Unnecessary items
- Upgrade more expensive gear slowly, like one per year
- Washing clothes vs. extra clothes
- Water sources: carrying vs. purifying
- Wood fuel vs. liquid fuel

Skills: Chapter Review

Chapter Summary

There are many skills for you to consider learning or improving.

- Safety, Leave No Trace (LNT) Ethics, First-Aid
- Navigation, Signaling, Survival
- Knot Tying, Bush Craft, Heat, Light
- Bug Protection, Toilet Time, Balance
- Weather Preparations for Rain, Snow, Cold, Hot, Dark

More Online: Backpacker.com has many articles to improve your skills.

Chapter Action Steps

☐ Evaluate your common practices against LNT Ethics.

☐ Take an online self-assessment for first-aid preparedness.

☐ Read up on navigation or signaling skills.

☐ Practice five knots until you can do them blindfolded.

☐ Name five methods for creating heat on a cold night.

☐ Update your supplies with updated bug repellents.

☐ Evaluate your gear based on the Balance section principles.

☐ Name five ways to keep warm or keep cool in the woods.

☐ If you find this book useful, look for other books in this Prep Lists Books series. Thank you!

Hard work pays off in the future. Laziness pays off now. ☺

Next Chapter

Now that you've mastered the skills needed to enjoy another outdoor adventure, let's review some checklists to be sure that you remember everything that you want and need while away from home.

Chapter 7. Checklists

Checklists: Chapter Intro

In this chapter, each checklist builds on the previous checklist. For example, 1) survival gear may be in your pants pockets, 2) hiking gear may add items in a fanny pack, 3) overnight backpacking gear may add items from fanny pack into a backpack, 4) week-long camping gear will add more equipment, etc. This chapter of checklists includes the following topics.

Checklists: Survival Gear Checklists

Introduction

These essential items should be taken with you any time you are in the woods, regardless of what you are doing or how long you plan to be there. These can be carried individually in your pockets, together in a kit, as a pouch in your backpack, or just a collection of things in your vehicle that is always ready to go.

Categories: The following types of items should be considered for any adventure into the wild.

- **Wallet:** Cash, credit cards, identification, emergency contact information, medicine information, health condition information, health insurance information, etc.
- **Keys** (steel or electronic): Security, access, protection, utilization
- **Mobile Device:** Cell phone for communication, GPS, maps, data
- **Blade:** Pocket knife, utility knife, hunting knife, or bowie knife
- **Cording:** Paracord bracelet or anklet, shoelaces, belt, knife grip
- **Fire Starting:** Lighter, fire steel, matches, lens, etc.
- **Lighting:** Flashlight, penlight, cell phone, fire starter, etc.
- **Weapon:** Knife, firearm, tactical light, pepper spray, Kubaton

Various Names (and associated abbreviations) are used for these items, depending on the context and expected use.

- Emergency Pouch
- Every Day Carry (EDC)
- Personal Survival Kit (PSK)
- Pocket Survival Kit (PSK)
- Survival Pack (Day Pack) or Survival Kit (Pocket Kit)

Sample Checklists: Rather than listing every possible item that might be in your core set of gear, here are several generic, representative samples to help you brainstorm on critical items for your particular activity, location, season, weather, and experience. Maybe none of these lists—by themselves—will suit you perfectly, but you'll get ideas about how to customize your own lists.

Day Kit Sample

This small pocket kit of essentials can go with you for any outdoor activity—whether hiking, cycling, hunting, fishing, camping, canoeing, skiing, four wheeling, rafting, or just climbing trees.

Fire

- Fire Starters: three methods for starting fires
- Pencil Sharpener: to create wood shavings for tinder

Water

- Zip-Tight Plastic Bags: for collecting water
- Purification Tablets: for bag of surface water

Emergency

- First Aid Kit: with antiseptic & bandages
- Whistle: to communicate with distant people
- Compass: to always know your bearings

Aim the hour hand of your analog wristwatch at the sun. Half way between the hour hand and 12 noon on your watch points south. The opposite points north.

Utility

- Aluminum Foil: for multiple uses
- Duct Tape: for multiple uses
- Fish Hooks and Fishing Line: for fishing and other utilization
- Knife: for multiple uses
- Paracord: for multiple uses

Overnight Kit Sample

This kit includes some basics for any overnight adventure.

Fire

- Dump Pouch: to gather fire starting materials or food
- Fire Starters: three methods for starting fires
- Large Knife: for splitting firewood into tinder and kindling

Water

- Bandana: for water filter and washcloth
- Metal Drinking Straw: to drink liquids from hot canteen
- Metal Water Bottle: for use in fire and in backpack

Other

- Metal tent pegs & wire mesh: for cooking over a fire
- Emergency Shelter: hammock, fly tarp, & paracord
- Knife sharpener: for safety and performance

*When prepping a bag for future or unplanned use,
remember to account for different seasons and temperatures.*

Multiple Night Kit Sample

This Survival Kit or Bug Out Bag (BOB) is always ready to go—by itself or to supplement other gear, depending on the context. Often there's room to include your day kit and overnight kit in the same bag—avoiding duplication of tools.

Fire

- Backup Fire Steel & Striker: for starting fires

Food

- Backup Mess Kit & Condiments: sugar, salt, coffee

Water

- Backup zip-tight plastic bags: for collecting water
- Backup Purification Tablets & Straw: for bag of surface water

Emergency Food

- Peanut butter: Three small jars = three days of calories
- Pocket fishing kit: for catching fish
- Rat trap with paracord: for catching small game or birds
- Snares & Extra Wire: for various utilization
- Air Rifle & box of 500 pellets: for survival hunting

Remember that hunting or fishing without a license usually requires a legitimate survival situation.

Other

- Crank-Powered Radio
- Crank-Powered Flashlight
- Toiletry Kit: with nail clippers, tweezers, toothbrush, etc.
- Extra Paracord: for multiple uses

Pocket Organizer Sample

Key categories in this kit include: shelter, fire, signaling, water, first aid, and utility.

Shelter

- Mylar Reflective Blanket
- Paracord
- Pocket Knife

Fire

- Fire Starters: three methods for starting fires

Signaling

- Bright yellow bandana
- Flashlight
- Glow stick
- Mirror
- Whistle

Water

- Aluminum Foil
- Purification Tablets
- Zip-Tight Plastic Bags

First Aid

- Gauze Pads & Duct Tape
- Lip Balm

Utility

- Notebook, sharpie pen, ballpoint pen, pencil

Every Day Pack & Pockets Sample

This is an example of what someone might use in daily adventures.

Pack

- Disinfectant Wipes
- Duct Tape wrapped around a gift card
- Emergency Whistle
- First Aid Kit: bandages, tweezers, clamps
- Flashlight
- Multi tool
- Pad of Paper with pencil or pen
- Pillbox with medicine and paracord lanyard
- Tape Measure: Retractable, 10-foot long, for bush craft
- Lighter: Stormproof with paracord lanyard & whistle
- Superglue: for gear repairs and wound closure
- USB flash drive

Pockets

- Cell Phone
- FitBit
- Flashlight
- Keys
- Paracord Bracelet
- Pocket Knife
- Space Pen
- Wallet
- Watch

Every Day Carry (EDC) Sample

Here are some basic tools that I may carry in my pockets for a quick hike in the woods—when I don't plan to be out for long, but I never know for sure.

Pockets

- Watch
- Wallet
- Keys
- Cell Phone (with map photos)
- Pocket Knife
- Firearm
- Lighter

Maybe Also...

- Pencil Sharpener (for making tinder out of sticks)
- Tactical Flashlight or Finger Light
- Backup battery charger for cell phone
- Bear Pepper Spray

If you fear confronting bear and considering taking a firearm, remember that Bear Pepper Spray is much lighter, much less expensive, and often more effective.

Pocket Survival Kit Sample

All of the following fit into large tin that can be added to any backpack, fanny pack, tackle box, or toolbox.

Fire

- Beeswax candle
- Bic mini lighter
- Fire steel - Ferro rod
- Fresnel Lens
- WetFire tinder

Tools

- Aluminum Foil – 2 feet
- Can opener
- Duct tape – 5 feet
- Flashlight Nano Light
- Leatherman multi tool
- Mini zip ties
- Nylon cording
- Ranger band
- S-Biner
- Sharpening stone
- Superglue
- Survival cards with instructions
- Tweezers

Hunting/Fishing

- Arrowhead/blade

Signaling

- Compass
- Mini signal mirror
- Paper & pen
- Whistle

First Aid Kit

- Alcohol swab

- Bandages
- Condom for water transport
- Bug/Insect repellent
- Medicine
- Neosporin
- Water purification tablets

Fishing Kit

- Bobbin of ten-pound fishing line
- Baits
- Hooks
- Snells
- Swivels
- Weights

Sewing Kit

- Bobbin of heavy duty sewing thread
- Button
- Needles
- Pins

Survival Sack Sample

These items could be combined with every day carry (EDC), camping gear, and a day pack. Priorities include 1) Fire, 2) Water, and 3) Rescue, signal, & navigation.

- Blaze Orange Cotton Bandana
- ChapStick lip balm
- Duct tape – 15 feet
- Expandable Sponge
- Heavy Duty Cording – 30 feet
- Orange Marking (Survey) Tape – 15 feet
- Paracord Lanyard – 8 feet
- Poncho & Gloves
- Ranger Bands
- Safety Pins
- Water Bags for water collection
- Water Straw for filtering drinking water

Survival Tin in waterproof, zip-tight plastic bags (protects smaller items)

- Bandages & alcohol prep pad
- Butane lighter
- Compass
- Cotton balls
- Fire steel & tinder
- Fresnel lens
- LED signal light
- Pocket knife multi tool
- Reflective tape – 3″x5″
- Signal mirror
- Survival kit labels with how-to information
- Water purification tablets
- Waterproof matches
- Whistle

Car Cache Sample

The following items might be kept in your vehicle for quick access.

Food & Water

- Several gallons of water
- Cooking Tin & a few days of non-perishable, nutritious food
- Water filtering and purification system
- Fishing or hunting equipment

Tools

- Compass
- Cording
- Duct Tape
- Fire starter
- Flashlight
- Knife
- Repair kit with safety pins

Medicine

- Pain Killers, Diarrhea Pills
- First Aid Kit: tweezers, bandages, antiseptic, tape, super glue

Other

- Butane lighter and matches
- Extra cash
- Extra clothing for warmth: gloves, hat, headband, socks
- Bug repellent
- Maps
- Mirror
- Paper and pen or pencil
- Plastic trash bags
- Reflective survival blanket
- Sunscreen or sunscreen spray
- Whistle
- Zip-Tight Plastic Bags

A DIY Tin Can Survival Kit Sample

Essentials

- Compass
- Extra clothing
- Extra food
- Fire starter
- First Aid Kit
- Flashlight with extra batteries
- Map
- Matches
- Pocket Knife
- Sunglasses

General

- Candle
- Cash
- Fire Starter/Tinder
- Fishing Line, Hooks, Sinkers
- Garbage Bags
- Knife
- Matches or Lighter
- Mirror
- Paper and Pencil
- Poncho
- Rope
- Surveyor's Tape
- Toilet Paper
- Whistle

Repairs

- Dental Floss
- Safety Pins
- Sewing Kit
- Wire

First Aid

- Aspirin
- Bandages
- First Aid Tape
- Moleskin
- Neosporin Antiseptic
- Sterile Gauze
- Sterile Pads

Nourishment

- Honey Packages
- Instant Soup or Tea

Optional

- Folding Saw
- Compass
- Hard Candy

While some kits are suited more toward personal comfort than just essentials for survival, feeling safe and comfortable are important survival assets.

Quick Reference List Sample

Fire, light, signaling, and heat

- Butane lighter, matches, fire steel, lens, etc.
- Flashlight, mirror, whistle, tape markers

Food and water

- Fishing gear
- Snare wire
- Dental floss
- Water purification
- Snack food: bouillon, hard candy, peanut butter
- Non-lubricated condoms: to store large amounts of water

Navigation

- Compass
- GPS device

Shelter

- Wood cutting tool
- Plastic bags, tarp, fly, poncho, or blanket

First Aid

- Antiseptic
- Wound treatment

Other

- Knife
- Sharpening stone
- Tweezers
- Information cards

Checklists: Hiking Checklists

This checklist for hiking includes topics not included in the previous **Checklists: Survival Gear Checklists** section of this chapter. In addition to tools and gear, consider these items.

Navigation

- Maps: paper, photos, GPS, smart phone, notes
- GPS devices, compass, smart phone apps
- Plan ahead
- Identify key milestones, landscape features, landmarks

Clothing

Before you go, plan for these.

- Change in temperature
- Change in weather
- Change in wind velocity or wind direction
- Change in terrain—hills, rocks, pavement, sand, mud, water
- Change in wet or dry trail conditions
- Change in snow cover
- Crossing water, swamp, or marsh
- Shoes or boots should be broken in to avoid blisters

Safety

Tell someone where you're going and when you'll be back.

- Phone a friend
- Send a text message
- Use a cell phone app that texts your GPS coordinates
- Leave a note on your car: where, why, how long
- Leave trail markers—which you collect on the return trip
- Warm up your muscles to avoid injury, especially when cold

Checklists: Backpacking Checklists

While every backpacking trek is different, here are some common items to consider taking with you. NOTE: "Backpacking" may also include hiking, camping, climbing, canoeing, kayaking, horseback riding, trail riding, ATV riding, snowmobile riding, cross-country skiing, rock climbing, spelunking, cycling, and more.

Category Quick Reference

- **Fire:** See Chapter 1 for more information
- **Water:** See Chapter 2 for more information
- **Food:** See Chapter 3 for more information
- **Shelter:** See Chapter 4 for more information
- **Clothing:** See Chapter 4 for more information
- **Sleeping:** See Chapter 4 for more information
- **Light:** See Chapter 4 for more information
- **Safety:** See Chapter 6 for more information
- **Survival Kit:** See Chapter 7 for more information

REI.com > Learn > Advice > Backpacking
is a great resource for beginners.

Safety

- **Tell Someone** where you're going and when you'll be back
- **Trip Itinerary**: locations & schedule, left with a friend & in car
- **Turn Back Time:** Determine safe TBT early and stick to it
- **Communication:** Cell phone, 2-way radios, AM/FM radio
- **Personal Defense Weapons:** Bear pepper spray, whistle, etc.
- **Maps:** Paper (in waterproof container), Smart Phone, GPS Device
- **Compass:** Magnetic, Smart Phone, GPS device
- **Watch:** Know time you've gone, time to return, time to sunset
- **Group:** Prepare an Emergency Response Plan for the group that includes itinerary, destination, dates, group members' emergency contacts, alternate meeting locations, etc.
- **Plan Ahead:** Know the names and locations of all nearby trails, roads, streams, and towns

Pack & Storage

- **Backpack:** your largest, primary pack (larger needed in winter)
- **Daypack, Summit Pack, or Fanny Pack:** for short hikes away from camp or in summer when little gear is needed
- **Pack Cover** for rain protection
- **Attachments:** D-Rings, bungee cords, or shock cording
- **Bear Canister** or hang bag & rope
- **Stuff Sacks** for compression or water protection

Put on your loaded backpack before you leave home. Be sure everything fits inside and that it's not too heavy. Typically your pack should be less than 25% of your body weight. Less than 20% is better. Up to 30% if needed for a short time.

Survival Kit

- Cell Phone: with waterproof bag and map photos
- Compass: to always know your bearings
- Duct Tape: for multiple uses
- Fire Starters: three methods for starting fires
- First Aid Kit: with antiseptic & bandages
- Knife: for multiple uses
- Mylar Reflective Blanket: for multiple uses
- Paracord: for multiple uses
- Purification Tablets: for bag of surface water
- Tactical Flashlight or Finger Light
- Whistle: to communicate with distant people
- Zip-Tight Plastic Bags: for collecting water

*The more extreme and remote your location will be,
the more extreme your gear and safety measures should be.
Do you need a Satellite Phone, Locator Beacon, Ice Axe, or Crampons?*

Water

- Water bottles, canteen, or bladder
- Water filtration, treatment, or purification system
- Drink Mixes: Lemonade, Kool-Aid, Tang, Punch, etc.

Plan to use between one half to one full gallon of water per person per day.

Food

- Meals and snacks
- Hot drinks: tea, coffee, hot chocolate, etc.
- Condiments
- Water for cooking
- Stove with fuel, windscreen, stand
- Cook Set, Dishes, Utensils, Cup
- Napkins or paper towels: for cleanup, padding, & insulating

Take extra rations in case your trip is unexpectedly extended. Consider peanut butter, energy/breakfast bars, jerky, nuts, or trail mix.

Shelter & Sleeping

- Tent or Bivy Sack with footprint, stakes, lines, etc.
- Hammock with straps & accessories
- Rain Fly or Tarp with lines
- Sleeping Bag, blanket, or quilt and pillow
- Sleeping Pad or foam or air mattress or ground cloth
- Sleeping Clothing
- Insect Netting

If you're new to backpacking, you probably do NOT want to take each item in this checklist. Instead, think of this as brainstorming ideas to consider and customize for your particular trip and personal needs.

Clothing

- **Think layers** of clothing rather than bulky options
- **Wicking** T-shirt, underwear, shorts
- **Plan to wash** a set of clothing if possible
- **Light Sandals** or flip flops are great when you arrive
- **Shoes or boots**, depending on the weather and terrain
- **Swimwear** if you might have the opportunity, or for bathing
- **Warm Clothing** if it may be cool: extra jacket, vest, sweatshirt, pants, gloves, hat, headband, balaclava, hand warmers
- **Backups** if you get wet: socks, gloves, underwear, etc.
- **Rainwear** for you and your pack

Personal

- Toilet Paper
- Lip balm (multiple utilizations)
- Hygiene Kit: toothbrush, soap, deodorant, toiletries
- Hand Sanitizer
- Insect Repellent
- Feminine hygiene products
- Glasses, Contacts/Solution, Medications, Supplements, etc.
- Sit Pad: Rectangular Sunshade Visor, with multiple utilizations

Light

- Flashlight
- Finger Light or Penlight
- Headlamp
- Lantern
- Smart Phone with flashlight function or flashlight app
- Maybe... extra batteries, a recharging battery for USB devices, or a solar panel for your backpack to recharge batteries

Sun Protection

- Hat with brim
- Bandana (multiple utilizations)
- Sunglasses
- Sunscreen lotion or sunscreen spray
- Nose cover (especially when on snow or water all day)

Other Possibilities

- Binoculars
- Bow Saw, folding saw, axe, hatchet, or batoning knife
- Fishing gear & license
- Gaiters
- Hunting gear & license
- Notebook journal or databook and writing instrument
- Park Permits
- Playing Cards or Games

- Reading Material: book, Kindle, cell phone app, eReader
- Repairs Kit: Knife, Multi Tool, Duct Tape, Spare Parts for gear
- Rope or Cording
- Trash/Garbage Bags
- Trekking Poles
- Towel for drying gear, cookware, or yourself after bathing
- Zip-Tight Plastic Bags: for food, clothing, gear, rain protection

If it has been a while, be sure all of your gear still works and in good condition before you go. A leaking tent or broken strap can ruin a trip.

Things You Don't Need

Consider making a list of luxury items that you really do not need to take on most trips. Think about items that you've packed before, but never used. Set them aside and pack them last. It's OK to take one or two non-essential things for your personal pleasure, but you also may enjoy a lighter, smaller pack.

Things to Do Before You Go

- Assemble or restock First-Aid Kit, Survival Kit, and Repair Kit
- Restock consumable supplies: toilet paper, sanitizer, lotions, etc.
- Purchase and pack stove fuel
- Exercise regularly to get into shape or stay in shape
- Practice your camping skills at home
- Read this book. Again.
- Wash, renew, and repair clothing, gear, bags, etc.
- Select, prepare, and pack clothing
- Research destination, route, alternate routes, parking, permits
- Capture map photos to smart phone
- Prepare Itinerary: one for friend and one for car
- Plan, purchase, prepare, & pack food
- Check weather forecast and update gear accordingly
- Recharge/replace batteries and battery recharger
- Pack bags
- Fill water containers
- Pack perishable foods

Checklists: Chapter Review

Chapter Summary

Compare various checklists to your trip, your destination, your group, and your personal preferences to decide what you most need.

- **Survival Gear Checklists:** Day Kit, Overnight Kit, Multiple Night Kit, Pocket Organizer, Every Day Pack, Every Day Carry, Pocket Survival Kit, Survival Sack, Car Cache, DIY Tin Can Survival Kit
- **Hiking Checklists:** Navigation, Clothing, Safety
- **Backpacking Checklists:** Topics, Safety, Gear, Things to Do

Chapter Action Steps

☐ Review these lists and highlight what you would use, or cross out what you would not use.

☐ Review these lists to create your own set of lists, based on the type of camping you are planning to enjoy.

☐ Review these lists to create your own lists, based on a summer, fall, winter, or spring hiking trip.

☐ Make a list of things to purchase or add to your gear.

☐ Make a list of things to learn more about.

☐ Review the Backpacking Checklists > Things to Do Before You Go and write in other activities that you would add to the list.

☐ If you find this book useful, look for other books in this Prep Lists Books series. Thank you!

The sooner you fall behind, the more time you'll have to catch up. ☺

Next Chapter

You are probably feeling ready to grab your gear and head out the door. Before you do, read one more chapter about resources available to you, so you can get the most out of your time away.

Chapter 8. Resources

Resources: Chapter Intro

This book does not have room for the many volumes of information related to camping, hiking, and backpacking. To help you find more detailed information, consider using the links in this chapter and online at PrepListsBooks.com to learn more.

This chapter on resources includes the following topics.

Please remember: mention of third parties or third-party products within this publication is for informational purposes only and constitutes neither a recommendation nor an endorsement. There are some links in this book that I may benefit from financially—with no higher prices or extra fees for you. Your support is appreciated.

Resources: Helpful Information

These resource links include a variety of helpful information related to topics in this book. These are educational for both novices and expert, and are particularly useful if you are new to camping and backpacking.

- Fire Safety when Building a Campfire at SmokeyBear.com
- Fire Safety at SmokeyBear.com
- Fire Safety at KidsCamping.com
- Fire Safety at PreventWildfireCA.org
- Fire Building: Tinder Finder at Backpacker.com
- Fire Building: Starting a Fire at Backpacker.com
- Fire Starting: Identifying Quartz at Geology.com
- Wilderness Survival at HowStuffWorks.com
- Eating Wild Plants at YouTube.com
- Switching from Tent to Hammock at TrekLightGear.com
- Shugemery's Hammock Camping Advice at YouTube.com
- Sleeping Bag Choices at REI.com
- Leave No Trace: Seven Principles at LNT.org
- Leave No Trace: Overview at Wikipedia.org
- Leave No Trace: Forestry Info at DCNR.PA.US
- Knot Tying Illustrations at Pinterest.com
- Uses for Paracord with Photos at Scribd.com
- Backpacker Skills Library at Backpacker.com
- Backpacking with Your Menstrual Period at REI.com
- Backpacking for Beginners at REI.com

If you are reading this as a printed book rather than a clickable eBook, see a list of link URLs in the next section, or visit PrepListsBooks.com > Resources > Links.

Resources: Online Products

These resource links provide quick access to various gear and products related to outdoor sports & recreation like camping, hiking, and backpacking.

- Outdoor Recreation
- Outdoor Clothing
- Outdoor Accessories
- Deals on Outdoor Sporting Gear
- Camping & Hiking
- Camping & Hiking > Backpacks & Bags
- Camping & Hiking > Tents & Shelters
- Camping & Hiking > Sleeping Bags & Bedding
- Camping & Hiking > Hammocks
- Camping & Hiking > Camp Kitchen
- Camping & Hiking > Freeze-Dried Food
- Camping & Hiking > Camping Furniture
- Camping & Hiking > Clothing
- Camping & Hiking > Footwear & Accessories
- Camping & Hiking > Hydration & Filtration
- Camping & Hiking > Knives & Tools
- Camping & Hiking > Lights & Lanterns
- Camping & Hiking > Headlamps
- Camping & Hiking > Navigation & Electronics
- Camping & Hiking > Personal Care
- Camping & Hiking > Insect Repellent
- Camping & Hiking > Safety & Survival
- Camping & Hiking > First Aid Kits
- Camping & Hiking > Emergency Fire Starters
- Camping & Hiking > Water Filters
- Camping & Hiking > Trekking Poles
- Camping & Hiking > Deals

If you are reading this as a printed book rather than a clickable eBook, see a list of link URLs in the next section, or visit PrepListsBooks.com > Resources > Links.

Resources: Link URLs

If you are reading this as a printed, paperback book rather than a clickable eBook, use this list of link URLs to access the underlined information links found throughout this book.

This same information is also an online resource page at PrepListsBooks.com > Resources > Links. By going to this one web page, you can then CLICK on any of the links in the following table (rather than typing them out). Check it out for quick access!

This table is a great Quick Reference to revisit linked information.

Page	Link Text	Link URL
	Intro	
1	PrepListsBooks.com	RockMediaPub.com/plb
2	PrepListsBooks.com > Resources > Links	RockMediaPub.com/resources/links
4	PrepListsBooks.com	RockMediaPub.com/plb
5	RockMediaPub.com/go/ToolsBonus	RockMediaPub.com/go/toolsbonus
21	PrepListsBooks.com	RockMediaPub.com/plb
21	feedback form	RockMediaPub.com/about/feedback
23	PrepListsBooks.com	RockMediaPub.com/plb
	Chapter 1. Fire	
33	electric generator	RockMediaPub.com/go/plb-powerpot
34	NPS.gov	RockMediaPub.com/go/plbi-nps-fire-conditions
34	tarp	RockMediaPub.com/go/plb-tarps
35	safely build your campfire	RockMediaPub.com/go/plbi-safe-campfire
36	Stoves for Cooking	RockMediaPub.com/go/plb-camp-stoves
36	SmokeyBear.com	RockMediaPub.com/go/plbi-smokeybear

Page	Link Text	Link URL
36	KidsCamping.com	RockMediaPub.com/go/plbi-kids-camping
36	PreventWildfireCA.org	RockMediaPub.com/go/plbi-prevent-wildfire
37	fire starters	RockMediaPub.com/go/plb-fire-starters
37	arc lighter	RockMediaPub.com/go/plb-arc-lighter
37	Rechargeable USB Lighter	RockMediaPub.com/go/plb-rechargable-lighter
37	Pocket torch lighters	RockMediaPub.com/go/plb-torch-lighters
37	Emergency Fire Starter kit	RockMediaPub.com/go/plb-zippo-lighter-kit
37	Lighters for Starting Fires	RockMediaPub.com/go/plb-fire-lighters
38	quartzite rock	RockMediaPub.com/go/plb-quartz
42	knife	RockMediaPub.com/go/plb-pocket-knives
42	zip-tight plastic bag	RockMediaPub.com/go/plb-ziplocbags
42	pencil sharpeners	RockMediaPub.com/go/plb-pencil-sharpeners
42	Cotton Balls	RockMediaPub.com/go/plb-cotton-balls
42	petroleum jelly	RockMediaPub.com/go/plb-petroleum-jelly
42	Cotton ball	RockMediaPub.com/go/plb-cotton-balls
42	zip-tight plastic bags	RockMediaPub.com/go/plb-ziplocbags
42	paraffin wax	RockMediaPub.com/go/plb-paraffin-wax
42	Cotton ball	RockMediaPub.com/go/plb-cotton-balls
42	zip-tight plastic bags	RockMediaPub.com/go/plb-ziplocbags
42	petroleum jelly	RockMediaPub.com/go/plb-petroleum-jelly
42	Cotton ball	RockMediaPub.com/go/plb-cotton-balls
42	petroleum jelly	RockMediaPub.com/go/plb-petroleum-jelly
42	paraffin wax	RockMediaPub.com/go/plb-paraffin-wax
42	paraffin wax	RockMediaPub.com/go/plb-paraffin-wax
42	Cotton	RockMediaPub.com/go/plb-cotton-balls

Page	Link Text	Link URL
42	Cotton Balls	RockMediaPub.com/go/plb-cotton-balls
42	heat fuel cans	RockMediaPub.com/go/plb-heat-fuel-cans
43	Trioxane	RockMediaPub.com/go/plb-trioxane
43	Never Dull	RockMediaPub.com/go/plb-never-dull
43	duct tape	RockMediaPub.com/go/plb-duct-tape
44	Cotton balls	RockMediaPub.com/go/plb-cotton-balls
44	sanitizer gel	RockMediaPub.com/go/plb-hand-sanitizer
44	Vaseline	RockMediaPub.com/go/plb-petroleum-jelly
44	wipe cloths	RockMediaPub.com/go/plb-sanitizing-wipes
44	bug repellent	RockMediaPub.com/go/plb-bug-repellent
44	Tinder Finder	RockMediaPub.com/go/plbi-backpacker-fire-tinder
46	saws	RockMediaPub.com/go/plb-folding-saw
46	Starting a Fire	RockMediaPub.com/go/plbi-backpacker-fire-starting
47	PrepListsBooks.com	RockMediaPub.com/plb
	Chapter 2. Water	
52	tarp	RockMediaPub.com/go/plb-tarps
54	Canteen	RockMediaPub.com/go/plb-water-canteen
54	Water Bladder	RockMediaPub.com/go/plb-water-bladder
54	Aluminum Foil	RockMediaPub.com/go/plb-aluminum-foil
54	Zip-Tight Plastic Bags	RockMediaPub.com/go/plb-ziplocbags
54	Trash Bags	RockMediaPub.com/go/plb-trash-bags
55	tarp	RockMediaPub.com/go/plb-tarps
57	Lifestraw Water Filter	RockMediaPub.com/go/plb-lifestraw
59	turkey-sized oven bags	RockMediaPub.com/go/plb-oven-bags

Page	Link Text	Link URL
61	turkey-sized oven bags	RockMediaPub.com/go/plb-oven-bags
62	plastic bag	RockMediaPub.com/go/plb-clear-trash-bags
62	large, clear, plastic bag	RockMediaPub.com/go/plb-clear-trash-bags
62	clear plastic sheet	RockMediaPub.com/go/plb-clear-trash-bags
63	clear plastic sheet	RockMediaPub.com/go/plb-clear-trash-bags
63	Wilderness Survival	RockMediaPub.com/go/plbi-howstuffworks-survival
64	household bleach	RockMediaPub.com/go/plb-liquid-chlorine-bleach
64	bleach	RockMediaPub.com/go/plb-liquid-chlorine-bleach
64	bleach	RockMediaPub.com/go/plb-liquid-chlorine-bleach
65	dry chlorine powder	RockMediaPub.com/go/plb-chlorine-powder
65	iodine bottles	RockMediaPub.com/go/plb-iodine-tablets
66	Water Purification Tablets	RockMediaPub.com/go/plb-water-pure-tablets
66	potassium permanganate	RockMediaPub.com/go/plb-potassium-permanganate
66	mechanical treatment	RockMediaPub.com/go/plb-water-filter-purify
67	UV water purifier lights	RockMediaPub.com/go/plb-uv-water-purifiers
69	writing a brief review	RockMediaPub.com/go/plb-kindle-book
69	Prep Lists Books series	RockMediaPub.com/plb
69	dehydrated water	RockMediaPub.com/go/plb-dehydrated-water
	Chapter 3. Food	
73	Ketchup & mustard	RockMediaPub.com/go/plb-ketchup-mustard
73	Hot sauce packets	RockMediaPub.com/go/plb-hot-sauce
73	BBQ sauce packets	RockMediaPub.com/go/plb-bbq-sauce
73	Mayo & relish packets	RockMediaPub.com/go/plb-mayo-relish

Page	Link Text	Link URL
73	Salt & pepper packets	RockMediaPub.com/go/plb-salt-pepper-packets
73	Sugar & sweetener packets	RockMediaPub.com/go/plb-sweetener-packets
73	Creamer & dried milk	RockMediaPub.com/go/plb-creamer-packets
73	Salad dressing packets	RockMediaPub.com/go/plb-salad-dressing-packets
73	Powdered drink mix	RockMediaPub.com/go/plb-punch-drink-mix
73	Lemon powder packets	RockMediaPub.com/go/plb-lemon-packets
73	air-tight container	RockMediaPub.com/go/plb-waterproof-dry-box
74	dry box	RockMediaPub.com/go/plb-waterproof-dry-box
74	ammo box	RockMediaPub.com/go/plb-ammo-box
74	cinch sack	RockMediaPub.com/go/plb-cinch-sac
74	zip-tight plastic bags	RockMediaPub.com/go/plb-ziplocbags
74	zip-tight plastic bags	RockMediaPub.com/go/plb-ziplocbags
74	zip-tight plastic bags	RockMediaPub.com/go/plb-ziplocbags
74	liquid soap	RockMediaPub.com/go/plb-hand-soap
74	Leather work gloves	RockMediaPub.com/go/plb-leather-gloves
74	vacuum sealing system	RockMediaPub.com/go/plb-vacuum-sealing-system
75	aluminum foil	RockMediaPub.com/go/plb-aluminum-foil
76	Jerky	RockMediaPub.com/go/plb-jerky
76	Sausages	RockMediaPub.com/go/plb-sausage-snacks
76	Pepperoni	RockMediaPub.com/go/plb-pepperoni-slices
76	Tuna Pouches	RockMediaPub.com/go/plb-tuna-pouches
76	Chicken Pouches	RockMediaPub.com/go/plb-chicken-pouches
76	Nuts & Seeds	RockMediaPub.com/go/plb-nuts
76	jars	RockMediaPub.com/go/plb-peanut-butter

Page	Link Text	Link URL
76	packets	RockMediaPub.com/go/plb-peanut-butter-packets
76	zip-tight plastic bag	RockMediaPub.com/go/plb-ziplocbags
76	Jelly Packets	RockMediaPub.com/go/plb-jelly-packets
76	Crackers	RockMediaPub.com/go/plb-crackers
76	peanut butter	RockMediaPub.com/go/plb-peanut-butter
76	Trail Mix	RockMediaPub.com/go/plb-trail-mix
76	Granola Bars or Mixes	RockMediaPub.com/go/plb-granola-mix
76	Energy Bars	RockMediaPub.com/go/plb-energy-bars
76	Protein Bars	RockMediaPub.com/go/plb-protein-bars
76	Fruit Cups	RockMediaPub.com/go/plb-fruit-cups
76	Applesauce Cups	RockMediaPub.com/go/plb-applesauce-cups
76	Pudding Cups	RockMediaPub.com/go/plb-pudding-cups
76	Dried Fruit	RockMediaPub.com/go/plb-dried-fruit
76	Dry Cereal Cups	RockMediaPub.com/go/plb-dry-cereal-cups
76	Crackers	RockMediaPub.com/go/plb-crackers
76	Peanut Butter Crackers	RockMediaPub.com/go/plb-peanut-butter-crackers
76	Pretzels	RockMediaPub.com/go/plb-pretzels
76	Snacks	RockMediaPub.com/go/plb-snacks
76	Cookies	RockMediaPub.com/go/plb-cookies
76	S'mores	RockMediaPub.com/go/plb-smores
77	Kool-Aid	RockMediaPub.com/go/plb-kool-aid
77	Crystal Light	RockMediaPub.com/go/plb-crystal-light
77	Gatorade Drink Mix	RockMediaPub.com/go/plb-gatorade
77	Punch Drink Mixes	RockMediaPub.com/go/plb-punch-drink-mix

Page	Link Text	Link URL
77	Lemonade	RockMediaPub.com/go/plb-lemonade
77	Tang	RockMediaPub.com/go/plb-tang
77	Nido dried milk mix	RockMediaPub.com/go/plb-nido-milk
78	tea	RockMediaPub.com/go/plb-adagio-tea
78	tea bags	RockMediaPub.com/go/plb-tea-bags
78	sweetener	RockMediaPub.com/go/plb-sweetener-packets
78	creamer	RockMediaPub.com/go/plb-creamer-packets
78	Hot chai spice powder mix	RockMediaPub.com/go/plb-chai-mix
78	Hot chocolate packets	RockMediaPub.com/go/plb-hot-chocolate
78	zip-tight plastic bag	RockMediaPub.com/go/plb-ziplocbags
78	Oatmeal	RockMediaPub.com/go/plb-oatmeal
78	Instant soup	RockMediaPub.com/go/plb-instant-soup
78	Ramen noodles	RockMediaPub.com/go/plb-ramen-noodles
78	Pasta sauce	RockMediaPub.com/go/plb-pasta-sauce-packets
78	Instant Potatoes	RockMediaPub.com/go/plb-instant-potatoes
78	Meals-Ready-to-Eat	RockMediaPub.com/go/plb-mre
78	zip-tight plastic bag	RockMediaPub.com/go/plb-ziplocbags
79	instant mashed potatoes	RockMediaPub.com/go/plb-instant-potatoes
79	dry milk	RockMediaPub.com/go/plb-nido-milk
79	Instant Vegetable Soup	RockMediaPub.com/go/plb-instant-soup
79	shredded chicken	RockMediaPub.com/go/plb-chicken-pouches
80	zip-tight plastic bag	RockMediaPub.com/go/plb-ziplocbags
80	zip-tight plastic bag	RockMediaPub.com/go/plb-ziplocbags
80	zip-tight plastic bag	RockMediaPub.com/go/plb-ziplocbags
80	Shugemery	RockMediaPub.com/go/plbi-shugemery

Page	Link Text	Link URL
81	Kelly Kettle	RockMediaPub.com/go/plb-kelly-kettles
81	Kelly Kettle Stainless Steel Medium Scout Basic Camp Stove Kit	RockMediaPub.com/go/plb-kelly-kettle-scout-kit
82	aluminum foil	RockMediaPub.com/go/plb-aluminum-foil
82	Dutch Oven	RockMediaPub.com/go/plb-dutch-oven
82	reflective oven	RockMediaPub.com/go/plb-reflective-oven
82	aluminum foil	RockMediaPub.com/go/plb-aluminum-foil
82	pressure cooker	RockMediaPub.com/go/plb-pressure-cooker
84	mountain pie makers	RockMediaPub.com/go/plb-pie-irons
85	Dutch Oven	RockMediaPub.com/go/plb-dutch-oven
85	aluminum foil	RockMediaPub.com/go/plb-aluminum-foil
90	edible plants images	RockMediaPub.com/go/plbi-pinterest-edible-plants
90	36 Wild Edibles	RockMediaPub.com/go/plb-wild-edibles-yt
90	cattails	RockMediaPub.com/go/plbi-plants-cattails
90	chickweed	RockMediaPub.com/go/plbi-plants-chickweed
90	chickweed online	RockMediaPub.com/go/plbi-plants-checkweek-video
91	clover	RockMediaPub.com/go/plbi-plants-clover
91	dandelion	RockMediaPub.com/go/plbi-plants-dandelion
91	Lamb's Quarters	RockMediaPub.com/go/plbi-plants-lambs-qtr
91	Wild Spinach	RockMediaPub.com/go/plbi-plants-wild-spinach
91	plantain	RockMediaPub.com/go/plbi-plants-plantain
91	thistle	RockMediaPub.com/go/plbi-plants-thistle
91	trillium	RockMediaPub.com/go/plbi-plants-trillium
91	Wild Edibles Identification	RockMediaPub.com/go/plb-wild-edibles-yt
91	edible plants book	RockMediaPub.com/go/plb-edible-plants-books

Page	Link Text	Link URL
95	make your own traps	RockMediaPub.com/go/plb-trap-snare-books
	Chapter 4. Shelter	
101	Feedback	RockMediaPub.com/about/feedback
102	tarp	RockMediaPub.com/go/plb-tarps
102	ridge tents	RockMediaPub.com/go/plb-tents-ridge
102	dome tents	RockMediaPub.com/go/plb-tent-dome
102	frame tents	RockMediaPub.com/go/plb-tent-frame
103	quick-pitch tents	RockMediaPub.com/go/plb-tent-quick-pitch
103	geodesic tents	RockMediaPub.com/go/plb-tent-geodesic
103	inflatable tents	RockMediaPub.com/go/plb-tent-inflatable
103	family cabin tents	RockMediaPub.com/go/plb-tent-family-cabin
103	tunnel tents	RockMediaPub.com/go/plb-tent-tunnel
103	pod tents	RockMediaPub.com/go/plb-tent-pod
104	tent repair kit	RockMediaPub.com/go/plb-tent-repair-kit
104	silicone spray	RockMediaPub.com/go/plb-silicone-spray
105	tarp	RockMediaPub.com/go/plb-tarps
106	Bivy bag	RockMediaPub.com/go/plb-bivvy-bag
106	sleeping platform	RockMediaPub.com/go/plb-sleeping-pads
106	insulated sleeping pads	RockMediaPub.com/go/plb-sleeping-pads
106	tarp	RockMediaPub.com/go/plb-tarps
106	blanket	RockMediaPub.com/go/plb-fleece-blanket
106	Reflective Car Sun Visor	RockMediaPub.com/go/plb-sunshade-visor
106	tarp	RockMediaPub.com/go/plb-tarps
107	sleeping bag	RockMediaPub.com/go/plb-sleeping-bag

Page	Link Text	Link URL
107	REI website	RockMediaPub.com/go/plbi-rei-sleeping-bags
108	Camping Pillows	RockMediaPub.com/go/plb-camping-pillows
108	zip-tight plastic bag	RockMediaPub.com/go/plb-ziplocbags
109	Switch from a Tent	RockMediaPub.com/go/plb-tent2hammock
109	hammock	RockMediaPub.com/go/plb-camping-hammocks
109	hammock with a screen	RockMediaPub.com/go/plb-camping-hammocks
109	rain fly	RockMediaPub.com/go/plb-hammock-rain-fly
109	small tarp	RockMediaPub.com/go/plb-hammock-rain-fly-picture
109	Hammock	RockMediaPub.com/go/plb-camping-hammocks
109	Sleeping bag	RockMediaPub.com/go/plb-sleeping-bag
109	Fleece liner	RockMediaPub.com/go/plb-fleece-blanket
109	flannel sheet	RockMediaPub.com/go/plb-flannel-sheets
109	Car shade visor pad	RockMediaPub.com/go/plb-sunshade-visor
109	Small utility bag	RockMediaPub.com/go/plb-utility-bag
109	Under Quilt	RockMediaPub.com/go/plb-hammock-under-quilt
109	Under Wrap	RockMediaPub.com/go/plb-sol-mylar-blanket
109	Tarp rain fly	RockMediaPub.com/go/plb-hammock-rain-fly
109	Hammock Hangin' How-To	RockMediaPub.com/go/plb-hammock-shugemery
110	paracord	RockMediaPub.com/go/plb-paracord4
110	bug netting	RockMediaPub.com/go/plb-hammock-bug-netting
110	under quilt	RockMediaPub.com/go/plb-hammock-under-quilt
110	under wrap	RockMediaPub.com/go/plb-sol-mylar-blanket
110	reflective car sun shade	RockMediaPub.com/go/plb-sunshade-visor
110	sleeping bag	RockMediaPub.com/go/plb-sleeping-bag

Page	Link Text	Link URL
110	over quilt	RockMediaPub.com/go/plb-hammocks-over-quilt
110	fleece blanket	RockMediaPub.com/go/plb-fleece-blanket
110	flannel sheet	RockMediaPub.com/go/plb-flannel-sheets
110	utility or ditty bag	RockMediaPub.com/go/plb-utility-bag
110	rain fly	RockMediaPub.com/go/plb-hammock-rain-fly
110	rain tarp	RockMediaPub.com/go/plb-hammocks-rain-tarp
110	Hammock Rain Fly	RockMediaPub.com/go/plb-hammock-rain-fly-picture
110	Hammock Under Quilt	RockMediaPub.com/go/plb-hammock-underquilt
110	Hammock & Mosquito Net	RockMediaPub.com/go/plb-hammock-bug-netting
111	Flashlight	RockMediaPub.com/go/plb-flashlight
111	Bug repellent	RockMediaPub.com/go/plb-bug-repellent
111	perimeter warning device	RockMediaPub.com/go/plb-laser-perimeter
113	sleeping bag	RockMediaPub.com/go/plb-sleeping-bag
113	flannel sheet	RockMediaPub.com/go/plb-flannel-sheets
113	fleece blanket	RockMediaPub.com/go/plb-fleece-blanket
113	Mylar emergency blanket	RockMediaPub.com/go/plb-sol-mylar-blanket
114	tarp	RockMediaPub.com/go/plb-tarps
114	reflective blanket	RockMediaPub.com/go/plb-sol-mylar-blanket
114	reflective blanket	RockMediaPub.com/go/plb-sol-mylar-blanket
114	tarp	RockMediaPub.com/go/plb-tarps
114	tent to a hammock	RockMediaPub.com/go/plb-tent2hammock
114	inflatable kiddie pool	RockMediaPub.com/go/plb-inflatable-pool
	Chapter 5. Tools	
121	Mylar	RockMediaPub.com/go/plb-mylar-blankets

Page	Link Text	Link URL
121	Emergency Blanket Options	RockMediaPub.com/go/plb-mylar-blankets
121	Heavy Duty Survival Blanket	RockMediaPub.com/go/plb-sol-blanket
123	flashlight	RockMediaPub.com/go/plb-flashlight
124	trash bags	RockMediaPub.com/go/plb-trash-bags
124	55-gallon drum liners	RockMediaPub.com/go/plb-55-gal-bags
124	Zip-Tight Plastic Bags	RockMediaPub.com/go/plb-ziplocbags
125	95-gallon trash bags	RockMediaPub.com/go/plb-95-gal-trashbag
125	Bivy bag	RockMediaPub.com/go/plb-bivvy-bag
127	tarpaulin	RockMediaPub.com/go/plb-tarps
127	tarp sizes, weights, and prices	RockMediaPub.com/go/plb-tarps
127	Trash Bag	RockMediaPub.com/go/plb-trash-bags
127	Mylar Blanket	RockMediaPub.com/go/plb-mylar-blankets
129	basic knot tying	RockMediaPub.com/go/plbi-knot-tying
129	Tactical Paracord Options	RockMediaPub.com/go/plb-paracord
132	101 Uses for Paracord	RockMediaPub.com/go/plbi-paracord-101-uses
132	bungee cord	RockMediaPub.com/go/plb-bungee-cord
132	shock cord	RockMediaPub.com/go/plb-shock-cord
133	rope	RockMediaPub.com/go/plb-rope
134	zip ties	RockMediaPub.com/go/plb-zip-ties
134	zip ties	RockMediaPub.com/go/plb-zip-ties
135	zip ties	RockMediaPub.com/go/plb-zip-ties
136	duct tape	RockMediaPub.com/go/plb-duct-tape
136	duct tape (DT)	RockMediaPub.com/go/plb-duct-tape
136	Duct tape	RockMediaPub.com/go/plb-duct-tape
137	zip-tight plastic bags	RockMediaPub.com/go/plb-ziplocbags

Page	Link Text	Link URL
139	Sunshade Visors	RockMediaPub.com/go/plb-sunshade-visor
149	coffee filters	RockMediaPub.com/go/plb-coffee-filters
150	aluminum foil	RockMediaPub.com/go/plb-aluminum-foil
151	flashlight	RockMediaPub.com/go/plb-flashlight
152	Hand Sanitizer	RockMediaPub.com/go/plb-hand-sanitizer
152	Super Glue	RockMediaPub.com/go/plb-superglue
152	single-use packs	RockMediaPub.com/go/plb-superglue
153	lip balm	RockMediaPub.com/go/plb-lip-balm-chapstick
158	zip-tight plastic bags	RockMediaPub.com/go/plb-ziplocbags
158	zip-tight plastic bags	RockMediaPub.com/go/plb-ziplocbags
158	Ziploc plastic bags	RockMediaPub.com/go/plb-ziplocbags
158	zip-tight plastic bag	RockMediaPub.com/go/plb-ziplocbags
160	writing a brief review	RockMediaPub.com/go/plb-kindle-book
160	Prep Lists Books series	RockMediaPub.com/plb
	Chapter 6. Skills	
165	flashlight	RockMediaPub.com/go/plb-flashlight
165	headlamp	RockMediaPub.com/go/plb-headlamp
165	sunscreen	RockMediaPub.com/go/plb-sunscreen-repellent
165	sunscreen spray	RockMediaPub.com/go/plb-sunscreen-spray
165	bug repellent	RockMediaPub.com/go/plb-sunscreen-repellent
166	zip-tight plastic bag	RockMediaPub.com/go/plb-ziplocbags
167	LNT.org	RockMediaPub.com/go/plbi-lnt
167	Leave No Trace	RockMediaPub.com/go/plbi-lnt-wiki
168	Forestry LNT	RockMediaPub.com/go/plbi-lnt-pa-forestry

Page	Link Text	Link URL
170	"Leave No Trace in the Outdoors"	RockMediaPub.com/go/plb-lnt-book-jm
171	first aid skills	RockMediaPub.com/go/plb-first-aid-skills
173	RedCross.org	RockMediaPub.com/go/plbi-red-cross
178	Headlamp	RockMediaPub.com/go/plb-headlamp
178	flashlight	RockMediaPub.com/go/plb-flashlight
179	Prep Lists Books series	RockMediaPub.com/go/amazonauthor-rk
179	survival skills	RockMediaPub.com/go/plb-survival-skills
181	basic knots	RockMediaPub.com/go/plb-knot-tying-books
181	knots to know	RockMediaPub.com/go/plb-knot-tying-books
183	bush craft	RockMediaPub.com/go/plb-bushcraft
183	bush craft books	RockMediaPub.com/go/plb-bushcraft
183	PrepListsBooks.com	RockMediaPub.com/plb
185	lantern	RockMediaPub.com/go/plb-lantern
185	flashlight	RockMediaPub.com/go/plb-flashlight
185	flashlights	RockMediaPub.com/go/plb-flashlight
185	headlamps	RockMediaPub.com/go/plb-headlamp
186	bug repellent	RockMediaPub.com/go/plb-bug-repellent
186	Permethrin	RockMediaPub.com/go/plb-permethrin
186	OFF! Deep Woods Insect Repellent	RockMediaPub.com/go/plb-off-deep-woods
186	Repel Natural Insect Repellent	RockMediaPub.com/go/plb-repel-insects
186	zip-tight plastic bag	RockMediaPub.com/go/plb-ziplocbags
186	Bug Wipes	RockMediaPub.com/go/plb-bug-wipes
186	Permethrin	RockMediaPub.com/go/plb-permethrin
186	ultrasonic repellent devices	RockMediaPub.com/go/plb-bug-ultrasonic-repellent

Page	Link Text	Link URL
186	personal clip-on mosquito repellent	RockMediaPub.com/go/plb-bugs-clip-on-repellent
186	batteries	RockMediaPub.com/go/batteries
186	Thermacell mosquito-repellant	RockMediaPub.com/go/plb-bugs-thermacell
187	bug repellent bracelets	RockMediaPub.com/go/plb-bug-bracelets
187	Thermacell mosquito-repellant	RockMediaPub.com/go/plb-bugs-thermacell
188	bug repellent for dogs	RockMediaPub.com/go/plb-bugs-dogs-repellent
189	zip-tight plastic bag	RockMediaPub.com/go/plb-ziplocbags
189	travel tissue packs	RockMediaPub.com/go/plb-travel-tissue-packs
190	zip-tight plastic bags	RockMediaPub.com/go/plb-ziplocbags
190	waste kit or WAG Bag	RockMediaPub.com/go/plb-waste-kit-wag-bag
190	menstrual options	RockMediaPub.com/go/plbi-periods
190	re-usable cup	RockMediaPub.com/go/plb-menstrual-cup
191	talcum powder	RockMediaPub.com/go/plb-talcum-powder
191	cornstarch	RockMediaPub.com/go/plb-cornstarch
191	zip-tight plastic bags	RockMediaPub.com/go/plb-ziplocbags
191	compactor trash bags	RockMediaPub.com/go/plb-compactor-bags
191	dry bag/box	RockMediaPub.com/go/plb-waterproof-dry-box
192	tarp	RockMediaPub.com/go/plb-tarps
192	tarps	RockMediaPub.com/go/plb-tarps
192	Hat	RockMediaPub.com/go/plb-hat-wide-brim
192	Umbrella	RockMediaPub.com/go/plb-pocket-umbrella
192	Jacket/Shell	RockMediaPub.com/go/plb-jacket-shell
192	Poncho	RockMediaPub.com/go/plb-poncho
192	Rain Pants	RockMediaPub.com/go/plb-rain-pants

Page	Link Text	Link URL
192	Boots	RockMediaPub.com/go/plb-waterproof-hiking-boots
192	Gaiters	RockMediaPub.com/go/plb-gaiters
192	Pack Cover	RockMediaPub.com/go/plb-pack-cover
192	Waterproof Stuff Sacks	RockMediaPub.com/go/plb-waterproof-stuff-sacks
192	Paracord	RockMediaPub.com/go/plb-paracord4
192	plastic bags	RockMediaPub.com/go/plb-ziplocbags
192	95-gallon trash bag	RockMediaPub.com/go/plb-95-gal-trashbag
192	tarp canopy	RockMediaPub.com/go/plb-tarps
192	Camp Dry Water Repellent	RockMediaPub.com/go/plb-camp-dry-water-repellent
194	car visor shade	RockMediaPub.com/go/plb-sunshade-visor
195	fleece	RockMediaPub.com/go/plb-fleece-blanket
195	flannel	RockMediaPub.com/go/plb-flannel-sheets
196	hand and foot warmers	RockMediaPub.com/go/plb-hand-warmer
196	folding hand saw	RockMediaPub.com/go/plb-folding-saw
196	pocket chain saws	RockMediaPub.com/go/plb-pocket-chain-saw
196	Car Reflector Visors	RockMediaPub.com/go/plb-sunshade-visor
196	oven bags	RockMediaPub.com/go/plb-oven-bags
196	zip-tight plastic bags	RockMediaPub.com/go/plb-ziplocbags
197	zip-tight plastic bag	RockMediaPub.com/go/plb-ziplocbags
197	lotion	RockMediaPub.com/go/plb-sunscreen-repellent
197	sunscreen spray	RockMediaPub.com/go/plb-sunscreen-spray
197	solar oven	RockMediaPub.com/go/plb-reflective-oven
198	space blanket	RockMediaPub.com/go/plb-mylar-blankets
198	Mesh Cot	RockMediaPub.com/go/plb-mesh-cot

Page	Link Text	Link URL
199	flashlight	RockMediaPub.com/go/plb-flashlight
199	flashlight	RockMediaPub.com/go/plb-flashlight
199	batteries	RockMediaPub.com/go/batteries
200	Flashlights	RockMediaPub.com/go/plb-flashlight
200	head-mounted flashlights	RockMediaPub.com/go/plb-headlamp
200	Lantern lights	RockMediaPub.com/go/plb-lantern
201	zip-tight plastic bags	RockMediaPub.com/go/plb-ziplocbags
201	bug repellent	RockMediaPub.com/go/plb-bug-repellent
201	sunscreen	RockMediaPub.com/go/plb-sunscreen-repellent
202	zip-tight plastic bags	RockMediaPub.com/go/plb-ziplocbags
203	Batteries	RockMediaPub.com/go/batteries
203	trash bag	RockMediaPub.com/go/plb-clear-trash-bags
203	Sleeping bag	RockMediaPub.com/go/plb-sleeping-bag
203	Tarp ground sheets	RockMediaPub.com/go/plb-tarps
203	Tyvek sheets	RockMediaPub.com/go/plb-tyvek
203	Tarps	RockMediaPub.com/go/plb-tarps
203	Rainflies	RockMediaPub.com/go/plb-hammock-rain-fly
203	Tent	RockMediaPub.com/go/plb-tent-dome
203	hammock	RockMediaPub.com/go/plb-camping-hammocks
203	Bivy	RockMediaPub.com/go/plb-bivvy-bag
203	carrying	RockMediaPub.com/go/plb-water-canteen
203	purifying	RockMediaPub.com/go/plb-water-filter-purify
204	Backpacker.com	RockMediaPub.com/go/plbi-backpacker-skills
204	Prep Lists Books series	RockMediaPub.com/plb

Page	Link Text	Link URL
Chapter 7. Checklists		
208	Pocket knife	RockMediaPub.com/go/plb-folding-knife
208	Paracord	RockMediaPub.com/go/plb-paracord
208	Lighter	RockMediaPub.com/go/plb-fire-lighters
208	Flashlight	RockMediaPub.com/go/plb-flashlight
208	Knife	RockMediaPub.com/go/plb-folding-knife
208	Emergency Pouch	RockMediaPub.com/go/plb-emergency-pouch
208	Every Day Carry (EDC)	RockMediaPub.com/go/plb-every-day-carry
208	Personal Survival Kit (PSK)	RockMediaPub.com/go/plb-personal-survival-kit
208	Pocket Survival Kit (PSK)	RockMediaPub.com/go/plb-pocket-survival-kit
208	Survival Pack	RockMediaPub.com/go/plb-survival-pack
208	Survival Kit	RockMediaPub.com/go/plb-survival-kit
209	Fire Starters	RockMediaPub.com/go/plb-fire-lighters
209	Zip-Tight Plastic Bags	RockMediaPub.com/go/plb-ziplocbags
209	Purification Tablets	RockMediaPub.com/go/plb-water-pure-tablets
209	First Aid Kit	RockMediaPub.com/go/plb-first-aid-kit
209	Whistle	RockMediaPub.com/go/plb-whistle
209	Compass	RockMediaPub.com/go/plb-compass
209	Aluminum Foil	RockMediaPub.com/go/plb-aluminum-foil
209	Duct Tape	RockMediaPub.com/go/plb-duct-tape
209	Knife	RockMediaPub.com/go/plb-folding-knife
209	Paracord	RockMediaPub.com/go/plb-paracord
210	Fire Starters	RockMediaPub.com/go/plb-fire-lighters
210	Large Knife	RockMediaPub.com/go/plb-folding-knife

Page	Link Text	Link URL
210	paracord	RockMediaPub.com/go/plb-paracord
211	zip-tight plastic bags	RockMediaPub.com/go/plb-ziplocbags
211	Purification Tablets	RockMediaPub.com/go/plb-water-pure-tablets
211	Crank-Powered Radio	RockMediaPub.com/go/plb-radio-crank-powered
211	Crank-Powered Flashlight	RockMediaPub.com/go/plb-flashlight-crank-powered
211	Paracord	RockMediaPub.com/go/plb-paracord
212	Mylar Reflective Blanket	RockMediaPub.com/go/plb-mylar-blankets
212	Paracord	RockMediaPub.com/go/plb-paracord
212	Pocket Knife	RockMediaPub.com/go/plb-folding-knife
212	Fire Starters	RockMediaPub.com/go/plb-fire-lighters
212	Flashlight	RockMediaPub.com/go/plb-flashlight
212	Whistle	RockMediaPub.com/go/plb-whistle
212	Aluminum Foil	RockMediaPub.com/go/plb-aluminum-foil
212	Purification Tablets	RockMediaPub.com/go/plb-water-pure-tablets
212	Zip-Tight Plastic Bags	RockMediaPub.com/go/plb-ziplocbags
212	Duct Tape	RockMediaPub.com/go/plb-duct-tape
212	Lip Balm	RockMediaPub.com/go/plb-lip-balm-chapstick
213	Duct Tape	RockMediaPub.com/go/plb-duct-tape
213	Whistle	RockMediaPub.com/go/plb-whistle
213	First Aid Kit	RockMediaPub.com/go/plb-first-aid-kit
213	Flashlight	RockMediaPub.com/go/plb-flashlight
213	Lighter	RockMediaPub.com/go/plb-zippo-lighter-kit
213	Flashlight	RockMediaPub.com/go/plb-flashlight
213	Paracord	RockMediaPub.com/go/plb-paracord

Page	Link Text	Link URL
213	Pocket Knife	RockMediaPub.com/go/plb-folding-knife
214	Pocket Knife	RockMediaPub.com/go/plb-folding-knife
214	Lighter	RockMediaPub.com/go/plb-zippo-lighter-kit
214	Flashlight	RockMediaPub.com/go/plb-flashlight
214	Finger Light	RockMediaPub.com/go/plb-finger-light
215	lighter	RockMediaPub.com/go/plb-fire-lighters
215	Aluminum Foil	RockMediaPub.com/go/plb-aluminum-foil
215	Duct tape	RockMediaPub.com/go/plb-duct-tape
215	cording	RockMediaPub.com/go/plb-paracord
215	Superglue	RockMediaPub.com/go/plb-superglue
215	Compass	RockMediaPub.com/go/plb-compass
215	Whistle	RockMediaPub.com/go/plb-whistle
216	Bug/Insect repellent	RockMediaPub.com/go/plb-bug-repellent
216	Water purification tablets	RockMediaPub.com/go/plb-water-pure-tablets
217	ChapStick lip balm	RockMediaPub.com/go/plb-lip-balm-chapstick
217	Duct tape	RockMediaPub.com/go/plb-duct-tape
217	Cording	RockMediaPub.com/go/plb-paracord
217	Paracord	RockMediaPub.com/go/plb-paracord
217	zip-tight plastic bags	RockMediaPub.com/go/plb-ziplocbags
217	lighter	RockMediaPub.com/go/plb-fire-lighters
217	Compass	RockMediaPub.com/go/plb-compass
217	Pocket knife	RockMediaPub.com/go/plb-folding-knife
217	Water purification tablets	RockMediaPub.com/go/plb-water-pure-tablets
217	Whistle	RockMediaPub.com/go/plb-whistle
218	Compass	RockMediaPub.com/go/plb-compass

Page	Link Text	Link URL
218	Cording	RockMediaPub.com/go/plb-paracord
218	Duct Tape	RockMediaPub.com/go/plb-duct-tape
218	Fire starter	RockMediaPub.com/go/plb-fire-lighters
218	Flashlight	RockMediaPub.com/go/plb-flashlight
218	Knife	RockMediaPub.com/go/plb-folding-knife
218	First Aid Kit	RockMediaPub.com/go/plb-first-aid-kit
218	lighter	RockMediaPub.com/go/plb-fire-lighters
218	Bug repellent	RockMediaPub.com/go/plb-bug-repellent
218	Plastic trash bags	RockMediaPub.com/go/plb-trash-bags
218	Reflective survival blanket	RockMediaPub.com/go/plb-mylar-blankets
218	Sunscreen	RockMediaPub.com/go/plb-sunscreen-repellent
218	sunscreen spray	RockMediaPub.com/go/plb-sunscreen-spray
218	Whistle	RockMediaPub.com/go/plb-whistle
218	Zip-Tight Plastic Bags	RockMediaPub.com/go/plb-ziplocbags
219	Compass	RockMediaPub.com/go/plb-compass
219	Fire starter	RockMediaPub.com/go/plb-fire-lighters
219	First Aid Kit	RockMediaPub.com/go/plb-first-aid-kit
219	Flashlight	RockMediaPub.com/go/plb-flashlight
219	batteries	RockMediaPub.com/go/batteries
219	Pocket Knife	RockMediaPub.com/go/plb-folding-knife
219	Fire Starter	RockMediaPub.com/go/plb-fire-lighters
219	Garbage Bags	RockMediaPub.com/go/plb-trash-bags
219	Knife	RockMediaPub.com/go/plb-folding-knife
219	Rope	RockMediaPub.com/go/plb-rope
219	Whistle	RockMediaPub.com/go/plb-whistle

Page	Link Text	Link URL
220	Compass	RockMediaPub.com/go/plb-compass
221	lighter	RockMediaPub.com/go/plb-fire-lighters
221	Flashlight	RockMediaPub.com/go/plb-flashlight
221	whistle	RockMediaPub.com/go/plb-whistle
221	Water purification	RockMediaPub.com/go/plb-water-pure-tablets
221	Compass	RockMediaPub.com/go/plb-compass
221	blanket	RockMediaPub.com/go/plb-fleece-blanket
221	Knife	RockMediaPub.com/go/plb-folding-knife
223	REI.com > Learn > Advice > Backpacking	RockMediaPub.com/go/plbi-rei-backpacking
224	Compass	RockMediaPub.com/go/plb-compass
224	Duct Tape	RockMediaPub.com/go/plb-duct-tape
224	Fire Starters	RockMediaPub.com/go/plb-fire-lighters
224	First Aid Kit	RockMediaPub.com/go/plb-first-aid-kit
224	Knife	RockMediaPub.com/go/plb-folding-knife
224	Mylar Reflective Blanket	RockMediaPub.com/go/plb-mylar-blankets
224	Paracord	RockMediaPub.com/go/plb-paracord
224	Purification Tablets	RockMediaPub.com/go/plb-water-pure-tablets
224	Flashlight	RockMediaPub.com/go/plb-flashlight
224	Finger Light	RockMediaPub.com/go/plb-finger-light
224	Whistle	RockMediaPub.com/go/plb-whistle
224	Zip-Tight Plastic Bags	RockMediaPub.com/go/plb-ziplocbags
226	Insect Repellent	RockMediaPub.com/go/plb-bug-repellent
226	Sunshade Visor	RockMediaPub.com/go/plb-sunshade-visor
226	Flashlight	RockMediaPub.com/go/plb-flashlight

Page	Link Text	Link URL
226	Finger Light	RockMediaPub.com/go/plb-finger-light
226	Headlamp	RockMediaPub.com/go/plb-headlamp
226	Lantern	RockMediaPub.com/go/plb-lantern
226	Sunscreen	RockMediaPub.com/go/plb-sunscreen-repellent
226	sunscreen spray	RockMediaPub.com/go/plb-sunscreen-spray
227	Knife	RockMediaPub.com/go/plb-folding-knife
227	Duct Tape	RockMediaPub.com/go/plb-duct-tape
227	Trash/Garbage Bags	RockMediaPub.com/go/plb-trash-bags
227	Zip-Tight Plastic Bags	RockMediaPub.com/go/plb-ziplocbags
228	Prep Lists Books series	RockMediaPub.com/plb

Chapter 8. Resources

Page	Link Text	Link URL
230	PrepListsBooks.com	RockMediaPub.com/resources
231	Fire Safety when Building a Campfire at SmokeyBear.com	RockMediaPub.com/go/plbi-safe-campfire
231	Fire Safety at SmokeyBear.com	RockMediaPub.com/go/plbi-smokeybear
231	Fire Safety at KidsCamping.com	RockMediaPub.com/go/plbi-kids-camping
231	Fire Safety at PreventWildfireCA.org	RockMediaPub.com/go/plbi-prevent-wildfire
231		RockMediaPub.com/go/plbi-backpacker-fire-tinder
231	Fire Building: Starting a Fire at Backpacker.com	RockMediaPub.com/go/plbi-backpacker-fire-starting
231	Fire Starting: Identifying Quartz at Geology.com	RockMediaPub.com/go/plb-quartz
231	Wilderness Survival at HowStuffWorks.com	RockMediaPub.com/go/plbi-howstuffworks-survival
231	Eating Wild Plants at YouTube.com	RockMediaPub.com/go/plb-wild-edibles-yt
231	Switching from Tent to Hammock at TrekLightGear.com	RockMediaPub.com/go/plb-tent2hammock

Page	Link Text	Link URL
231	Shugemery's Hammock Camping Advice at YouTube.com	RockMediaPub.com/go/plbi-shugemery
231	Sleeping Bag Choices at REI.com	RockMediaPub.com/go/plbi-rei-sleeping-bags
231	Leave No Trace: Seven Principles at LNT.org	RockMediaPub.com/go/plbi-lnt
231	Leave No Trace: Overview at Wikipedia.org	RockMediaPub.com/go/plbi-lnt-wiki
231	Leave No Trace: Forestry Info at DCNR.PA.US	RockMediaPub.com/go/plbi-lnt-pa-forestry
231	Knot Tying Illustrations at Pinterest.com	RockMediaPub.com/go/plbi-knot-tying
231	Uses for Paracord with Photos at Scribd.com	RockMediaPub.com/go/plbi-paracord-101-uses
231	Backpacker Skills Library at Backpacker.com	RockMediaPub.com/go/plbi-backpacker-skills
231	Backpacking with Your Menstrual Period at REI.com	RockMediaPub.com/go/plbi-periods
231	Backpacking for Beginners at REI.com	RockMediaPub.com/go/plbi-rei-backpacking
231	PrepListsBooks.com > Resources > Links	RockMediaPub.com/resources/links
232	Outdoor Recreation	RockMediaPub.com/go/plb8-outdoor-recreation
232	Outdoor Clothing	RockMediaPub.com/go/plb8-outdoor-clothing
232	Outdoor Accessories	RockMediaPub.com/go/plb8-outdoor-accessories
232	Deals on Outdoor Sporting Gear	RockMediaPub.com/go/plb8-outdoors-deals-sporting-gear
232	Camping & Hiking	RockMediaPub.com/go/plb8-outdoors-camping-hiking
232	Camping & Hiking > Backpacks & Bags	RockMediaPub.com/go/plb8-outdoor-ch-backpacks-bags
232	Camping & Hiking > Tents & Shelters	RockMediaPub.com/go/plb8-outdoor-ch-tents-shelters
232	Camping & Hiking > Sleeping Bags & Bedding	RockMediaPub.com/go/plb8-outdoor-ch-sleeping-bags-bedding
232	Camping & Hiking > Hammocks	RockMediaPub.com/go/plb8-outdoor-ch-hammocks

Page	Link Text	Link URL
232	Camping & Hiking > Camp Kitchen	RockMediaPub.com/go/plb8-outdoor-ch-camp-kitchen
232	Camping & Hiking > Freeze-Dried Food	RockMediaPub.com/go/plb8-outdoor-ch-freeze-dried-food
232	Camping & Hiking > Camping Furniture	RockMediaPub.com/go/plb8-outdoor-ch-camping-furniture
232	Camping & Hiking > Clothing	RockMediaPub.com/go/plb8-outdoor-ch-clothing
232	Camping & Hiking > Footwear & Accessories	RockMediaPub.com/go/plb8-outdoor-ch-footwear-accessories
232	Camping & Hiking > Hydration & Filtration	RockMediaPub.com/go/plb8-outdoor-ch-hydration-filtration
232	Camping & Hiking > Knives & Tools	RockMediaPub.com/go/plb8-outdoor-ch-knives-tools
232	Camping & Hiking > Lights & Lanterns	RockMediaPub.com/go/plb8-outdoor-ch-lights-lanterns
232	Camping & Hiking > Headlamps	RockMediaPub.com/go/plb8-outdoor-ch-headlamps
232	Camping & Hiking > Navigation & Electronics	RockMediaPub.com/go/plb8-outdoor-ch-navigation-electronics
232	Camping & Hiking > Personal Care	RockMediaPub.com/go/plb8-outdoor-ch-personal-care
232	Camping & Hiking > Insect Repellent	RockMediaPub.com/go/plb8-outdoor-ch-insect-repellent
232	Camping & Hiking > Safety & Survival	RockMediaPub.com/go/plb8-outdoor-ch-safety-survival
232	Camping & Hiking > First Aid Kits	RockMediaPub.com/go/plb8-outdoor-ch-first-aid-kits
232	Camping & Hiking > Emergency Fire Starters	RockMediaPub.com/go/plb8-outdoor-ch-fire-starters
232	Camping & Hiking > Water Filters	RockMediaPub.com/go/plb8-outdoor-ch-water-filters
232	Camping & Hiking > Trekking Poles	RockMediaPub.com/go/plb8-outdoor-ch-trekking-poles
232	Camping & Hiking > Deals	RockMediaPub.com/go/plb8-outdoor-ch-deals
232	PrepListsBooks.com > Resources > Links	RockMediaPub.com/resources/links
233	PrepListsBooks.com > Resources > Links	RockMediaPub.com/resources/links

Page	Link Text	Link URL
259	PrepListsBooks.com	RockMediaPub.com/plb
259	feedback form	RockMediaPub.com/about/feedback
260	feedback form	RockMediaPub.com/about/feedback
	Chapter 9. Heading Out	
261	PrepListsBooks.com	RockMediaPub.com/plb
262	this book at Amazon	RockMediaPub.com/go/amazonbook-pl4chb
262	this book at Amazon	RockMediaPub.com/go/amazonbook-pl4chb
262	Prep Lists Books at Amazon	RockMediaPub.com/go/plb-kindle-books
262	books by the same author	RockMediaPub.com/go/amazonauthor-rk
262	PrepListsBooks.com	RockMediaPub.com/plb
262	PrepListsBooks.com	RockMediaPub.com/plb
262	this book at Amazon	RockMediaPub.com/go/amazonbook-pl4chb

Using the links from this book to retail web sites may benefit this book's author and publisher financially—with no higher prices or extra fees for you.
If you'd like a quick, easy way to demonstrate your support for this and similar books, please use these links any time you plan to make a purchase from these retail sites. Thank you!

Resources: Additional Content

The following topics are planned for future Prep Lists Books, which may be compiled into **Volume 2** of "Prep Lists for Camping, Hiking, and Backpacking," a second edition, or as online resources at PrepListsBooks.com. Please use the online feedback form to let me know what you think about these or other topics that you'd like to see in future books. Thanks.

Destinations

- National Parks & National Forests
- State Parks & State Forests
- Major Hiking Trails
- Other Outdoor Attractions

Fun Things to Do

- Photography & Videography
- Exploring & Geocaching
- Educational & Historical
- Botany (trees, edible plants, medicinal plants, etc.)
- Bush Craft Projects, Games, & Challenges
- More Checklists of things to take camping

Family Camping

- Safety First for Children
- Activities for Kids & Family
- Extra Gear for Youngsters & Pets
- Family Friendly Foods

Safety

- Basic Safety Measures
- Keeping Others Informed
- Bear and Wild Animals
- Recharging from Battery, Solar, Mechanical, or Heat

Resources: Chapter Review

Chapter Summary

Beyond this book there are so many more resources available for you to prepare for camping, hiking, and backpacking.

- Resource Links for **Helpful Information**
- Resource Links for **Buying Gear**
- Resource Links for **Product Information**
- Resource Links for **Additional Content** and future books

Chapter Action Steps

☐ Visit a few info links and explore new topics to learn.

☐ Visit a retail link to see what's new & compare models.

☐ Visit some product links to see what they look like, what options are available, and compare prices.

☐ Visit the feedback form link to let the author and publisher know what you'd like to see in future books.

I went to a bookstore and asked the sales-woman, "Where's the self-help section?" She said if she told me, it would defeat the purpose. ☺

Next Chapter

This book is full of so much information and links to so many resources that your brain is probably telling you to just get out of the house and go camping. So do it! Before you go, please read the last chapter, "Heading Out," with a personal message from the author.

Chapter 9. Heading Out

Thank You

I hope that you've enjoyed reading this book and found it as useful as I have. Thank you so much for your interest and support of the Prep Lists book series. I welcome your feedback about this, other, and future books at PrepListsBooks.com. Would you like another book with more of the same? Maybe a new book on a similar subject? Perhaps a different topic using the Prep Lists format? Please let me know! You can even sign up to be notified when new books and other resources become available.

Having completed this book, you should now feel prepared and ready to go—so head on out to enjoy the great outdoors and admire God's creation! Perhaps we will meet face-to-face on a hiking trail someday; be sure to introduce yourself. :-) Remember, wherever you go, that's where you'll be.

Ronald E. Kaine

Action Steps

☐ Visit this book at Amazon to write a book review. This is important because it helps both the publisher and the potential readers to better understand the value of the book.

☐ If you are reading this book on a kindle device or kindle software, when you turn to the last page of this book, you will have an opportunity to review it. Please do!

☐ Consider using your Kindle Reader's "share" function to let others know about this book and how much you liked it.

☐ If you received this book as a FREE promotion and you found it to be helpful to anyone who likes to go camping, hiking, or backpacking, then please consider writing a helpful review for this book at Amazon so others can benefit from it. Thank you!

☐ Look for other Prep Lists Books at Amazon.

☐ Look for other books by the same author at Amazon.

☐ Visit PrepListsBooks.com for any of the following.

- More info, links, demonstrations that didn't fit into this book
- See similar books in the Prep Lists Books series
- See books in other series by the same publisher or author
- Sign up for future book notifications
- Provide feedback & suggestions for future books

☐ Now, get outdoors and enjoy...

Remember

Please don't copy or distribute this book without permission. Much time and effort went into creating it, so please respect the author and the publisher by not sharing this book in any form. Instead, point others to PrepListsBooks.com or this book at Amazon so they can purchase a copy. Then both of us will benefit and say, "Thank you!"

28734486R00144

Made in the USA
Lexington, KY
19 January 2019